WORKING OUT OF THE BOX

ADVANCE PRAISE FOR THE BOOK

'*Working Out of the Box* is an excellent, thought-provoking read for any leader who wants to transform their culture and better understand how to shape their organizational environment. Aparna Piramal Raje demonstrates that *how* you work can be just as important as what you work on.'
Sarah Stein Greenberg, executive director, Hasso Plattner Institute of Design at Stanford University (the d.school)

'A masterful tour of the inner sanctums of successful C-suites, this book not only satisfies our curiosity about how these private spaces set the conditions for their occupants' success, but also highlights the small yet critical design elements—the artefacts and stories—that these leaders use daily to remind themselves who they are and present themselves to others. Each caselet makes you feel as if you have been inside both the leader's office and mind. The leaders, and their philosophies, become as authentically tangible as the spaces are real.'
Ethan Bernstein, assistant professor of leadership and organizational behavior, Harvard Business School

'Corporate India is an under-researched area in terms of workplace design. This accessible and informative book takes us inside the workspaces of forty Indian chief executives to explore the relationship between business motivation and working environment. A must-read for everyone interested in how the world of work is changing globally.'
Professor Jeremy Myerson, Royal College of Art, London

'Much attention is given to the public pronouncements of business leaders, but oddly little to their private working styles. *Working Out of the Box* is a timely correction, providing an insightful and fascinating peek behind the scenes of the corporate titans remaking modern India—and the way in which their offices and habits shape both the companies and industries they lead.'
James Crabtree, *Financial Times* (UK)

'Fulfilment, either as an individual or as a professional, comes from genuineness, rather than imposing a style on oneself. Ms Raje's sketches bring alive the core beliefs and sincerity with which they are living their lives.'
Ratan Tata, chairman, Tata Trusts

'Aparna Piramal Raje's new book on leadership and design is a collection of intriguing detective stories. She gathers evidence from the offices of a diverse group of chief executives to decode their secrets of business and personal success. Even things as mundane as the style of desks, bookcases and doors, or intangibles such as atmosphere, hold vital clues for the author. I was inspired by her revelations to take another look at my own work environment.'
Rakesh Kapoor, CEO of Reckitt Benckiser

'Aparna offers a unique view of how leadership traits are reflected in the way people organize their work environment and how it has been evolving with the years and generations. The impact that "entering into the leader's office" has on people is quite often underscored, but the book makes quite clear how much one can learn and create first impressions by doing that. Most definitely a refreshing point of view that should make us all reflect on what our office has to say about ourselves as leaders!'
Claudia Sender, CEO, TAM Airlines (Brazil)

'I have always enjoyed Aparna's unique style of journalism. She effectively blends a wide experience in design with an understanding of business, and insightful observations about people, to weave a colourful picture of each leader and their leadership style in the contexts of their different businesses. A refreshing approach to business journalism.'
Lakshmi Venu, joint managing director, Sundaram Clayton

WORKING OUT OF THE BOX

40 stories of leading CEOs

APARNA PIRAMAL RAJE

PORTFOLIO PENGUIN

An imprint of Penguin Random House

PORTFOLIO

USA | Canada | UK | Ireland | Australia
New Zealand | India | South Africa | China | Singapore

Portfolio is part of the Penguin Random House group of companies whose addresses can be found at global.penguinrandomhouse.com

Published by Penguin Random House India Pvt. Ltd
4th Floor, Capital Tower 1, MG Road,
Gurugram 122 002, Haryana, India

Penguin Random House India

First published by Random House India 2015
Published in Portfolio by Penguin Random House India 2019

10 9 8 7 6 5 4 3

The views and opinions expressed in this book are the author's own and the facts are as reported by her, which have been verified to the extent possible, and the publishers are not in any way liable for the same.

ISBN 9788184007350

Printed at Manipal Technologies Limited, India

www.penguin.co.in

FSC www.fsc.org MIX Paper from responsible sources FSC® C043100

To

{ Radhika Desai & Seema Chowdhry }
for fostering design thinking and writing

and

{ Mom & Amit }
for everything

TABLE OF CONTENTS

FOREWORD BY ANAND G. MAHINDRA xii

INTRODUCTION xiv

HOW THIS BOOK WORKS xix

I: PERSONAL ENERGY 1

Accessibility 4
Deepak Parekh, Housing Development Finance Corp. 5
Natarajan Chandrasekaran, Tata Consultancy Services 10

Learning & Renewal 15
Anil Khandelwal, ex-Bank of Baroda 16
Captain C.P. Krishna Nair, Leela group 21
Harsh Mariwala, Marico 26

Partnerships 31
Cyril & Vandana Shroff, Cyril Amarchand Mangaldas 32
Neera Nundy & Deval Sanghavi, Dasra 37
Vysyaprath Sunil & Mohit Dhar Jayal, Weiden + Kennedy 42

Portfolio lives 47
Prasoon Joshi, McCann Erickson 48
Rajagopalan Balakrishnan, Lowe Lintas 53
Tasneem Zakaria Mehta, Bhau Daji Lad 57

Resilience 62
Chitra Ramkrishna, National Stock Exchange 63
G.V. Sanjay Reddy, GVK Group 68
T.V. Narendran, Tata Steel 73
Vikram Limaye, Infrastructure Development Finance Corp. 78

Spirituality 83
Ajay Piramal, Piramal group 84
Kumar Mangalam Birla, Aditya Birla group 89

II: ORGANIZATIONAL CAPITAL 94

AGILITY 97
Lynda Gratton, London Business School 98
Subroto Bagchi, Mindtree 104
Vineet Nayyar, Tech Mahindra 109

COLLABORATION 114
Aruna Jayanthi, CapGemini 115
Shantanu Khosla, ex-Procter & Gamble 120
Shikha Sharma, Axis Bank 125

CRAFTSMANSHIP 130
Baba Kalyani, Bharat Forge 131
Rajiv Bajaj, Bajaj Auto 136
Ralf Speth, Jaguar Land Rover 141

INTEGRATIVE THINKING 146
Martin Sorrell, WPP 147
Rajan Anandan, Google 152

PURPOSE 157
Nitin Nohria, Harvard Business School 158
Uday Kotak, Kotak Mahindra 163

III: BRAND VALUES 168

INNOVATION 171
Kiran Mazumdar-Shaw, Biocon 172
Park Won-Soon, Mayor of Seoul 177

PERSONAL BRANDING 182
Kishore Biyani, Future Group 183
Rakesh Jhunjhunwala, Rare Enterprises 188

STORYTELLING 193
Amar Goel, Komli Media & Aditya Swamy, MTV 194
Anoop Prakash, Harley Davidson 200
Dippak Khurana, Vserv & Mukesh Bansal, Myntra.com 205
Rajiv Mehta, ex-Puma 211

IV: ENVIRONMENT & SUSTAINABILITY 216

SUSTAINABILITY 217
Douglas Baillie, Unilever 219
Meher Pudumjee, Thermax 224

ACKNOWLEDGEMENTS 229

ANSWERS TO THE WORKPLACE QUIZ & PHOTO CREDITS 232

ABOUT THE AUTHOR 233

Chairman & Managing Director
Mahindra Group

ANAND G. MAHINDRA

FOREWORD

Working Out of the Box is an original collection of forty profiles of chief executives in their workspaces. These fascinating pen portraits are like miniature paintings in their detail, intricacy and nuance. This book also innovatively explores the subtle connections between workspaces and work styles, which is a fresh and novel approach. There are three reasons I would urge you to read this book.

First, it offers lessons on leadership from a very diverse pool of subjects. There is a wide range of ages, sectors, geographies, industries and work styles represented, which gives readers a very wide-angle view of the way business works.

Second, this book brings out the very important connection between design and business results. Design is an intangible that is often overlooked. But I fully share the author's view that the design environment shapes people and hence shapes results. As the head of the India Design Council, I am particularly delighted to see the way business and design have been blended to deliver new insight into management thinking. The book's emphasis on connecting tangible workplace design with intangible assets is both compelling and differentiated.

Third, this book recognizes that workplaces are not just a form of capital expenditure, but that they are tangible tools, platforms and resources by which business leaders can influence work styles, leading to economic value creation. They are a form of communication about jobs, careers and livelihoods. Paying close attention to these aspects will be an important factor in harnessing India's demographic dividend.

I found this book both interesting and enlightening, and I am hopeful that it will create a change of thinking and attitudes in the everyday world of work.

INTRODUCTION

If you are reading this, you are interested in knowing more about corporate India. Could you guess which business leader(s):

1. Plays a game of Sudoku every night before going to bed?
2. Never uses a computer to write important thoughts?
3. Always work alongside their spouses?
4. Run the Indian arm of a large MNC but don't have private cabins?
5. Has a Rudyard Kipling poem next to his desk?
6. Had a fully fledged slide in his office?
7. Have Gandhian memorabilia in their offices?
8. Have extensive art collections at work?
9. Like to stand and work?
10. Videoconference daily?[1]

Business leaders are often assessed in terms of the big picture–their business strategy and vision, and their ability to drive change and deliver results. While these 'outside-in' descriptions may give an insight into their capabilities, they don't always capture their personality, their individual ways of working or the everyday nuances of their leadership abilities.

Inside-out portraits

The *Head Office* column began five years ago in the *Mint*, a business daily, in an attempt to distill how chief executives work–what they read, how they use technology, how they interact with their colleagues, and what motivates them –and to explore the connections between their work styles and workspaces.

I was keen to profile business leaders from the 'inside-out' and the goal was to present them at a human-scale, where readers feel as though they were standing next to them, in the corner office.

[1]Answers on page 232

It is apparent that India's business leadership is changing in visible ways. One size no longer fits all: the stereotypical image of a chief executive in a secluded corner office, disconnected from employees, is receding. Instead, a wide range of workplaces and work styles can be seen, including progressive leadership traits such as agility, craftsmanship and portfolio lives.

Over the course of fifty columns, companies of different scales–major to minor, across sectors and geographies–run by chief executives of differing ages and temperaments have been featured. The qualifying criteria included having a distinctive space, a unique way of working, and a compelling and credible business story.

A few caveats: From the original set of fifty interviews, I was unable to include in the book all those who were interviewed (although all are available online). Also, some cities are under-represented (not for lack of trying, in many cases).

Connecting business and design

Tangible assets, such as workplaces, represent substantial capital expenditure for any organization. Intangible assets, such as corporate culture or brand values, often account for the greater part of company valuation. Yet there is little research on the relationship between these two entities. So I wanted to interview chief executives in their personal spaces to decipher how tangible workplace assets related to intangible assets, and perhaps even to provide a simple framework for business leaders and architects to communicate better with each other.

In the course of the series, two findings emerged, which shed light on the connection between business and workplace design, as follows:

- **What your office says about you:** I noticed it was possible to classify CEO's private workspaces (or C-suites) into **four distinct workplace archetypes,** based on their design, usage and primary purpose. These workplace archetypes provide insight into a CEO's business priorities and personality.

- **How to manage intangible assets**: Certain patterns, namely **fifteen work styles,** or ways of working, could be noticed in the ways CEOs manage intangible assets. These work styles capture 'inside-out' nuances of their leadership traits and personality.

What your office says about you

As I conducted my interviews, I discovered that chief executives generally use their C-suites in one of four ways, depending on their primary purpose, usage and design.

For most chief executives, the C-suite is **an anchor to nourish their personal energy**. For many others, it is a tool to build **organizational capital**, i.e. work culture, structure and processes. Others leverage it as a platform to **communicate brand values**. And finally some have begun to think of workplaces as a resource, in terms of **sustainability and the environment**. Thus each C-suite can be categorized into a specific '**workplace archetype**', based on which of the four intangible assets it supports.

Of course there is substantial overlap for any given C-suite, as most chief executives will be interested in managing most, if not all, of these intangible assets. For example, several C-suites that I feel serve mainly as 'tools to build human capital' are also 'anchors to nourish personal energy'. What the grouping highlights is the primary purpose for a given C-suite and which intangible assets it primarily enhances.

Four workplace archetypes

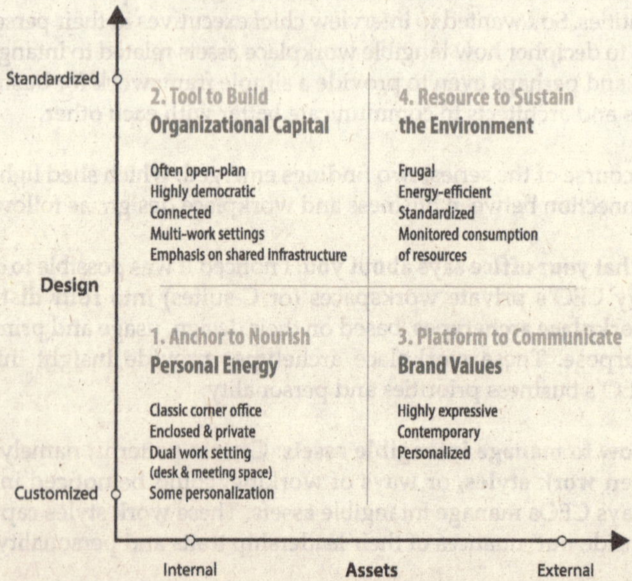

A C-suite's primary purpose is expressed through its workplace design, as shown in the chart below. For example, chief executives who are using their workplaces as a tool to build organizational capital or to sustain the environment, tend to have more standardized workplaces. Those who are using it to nourish personal energy, or to communicate brand values, tend to have more personalized workspaces.

Each workplace archetype is thus an expression of both the design characteristics and the business needs of a C-suite. In other words, the more we know about workplace design, the more we can learn about chief executives, their work styles, leadership traits and their business priorities.

Or, turning the argument on its head, if we can explicitly define business priorities, we can configure our work environments to better support them, and extract a greater return from our tangible infrastructure. Each C-suite thus has significant design implications, which are discussed at the beginning of each section, as well as in individual chapters.

How to manage intangible assets

Just as C-suites can be classified into one of four workplace archetypes, as I conducted my interviews, I noticed certain patterns in how

Workplace archetypes & work styles

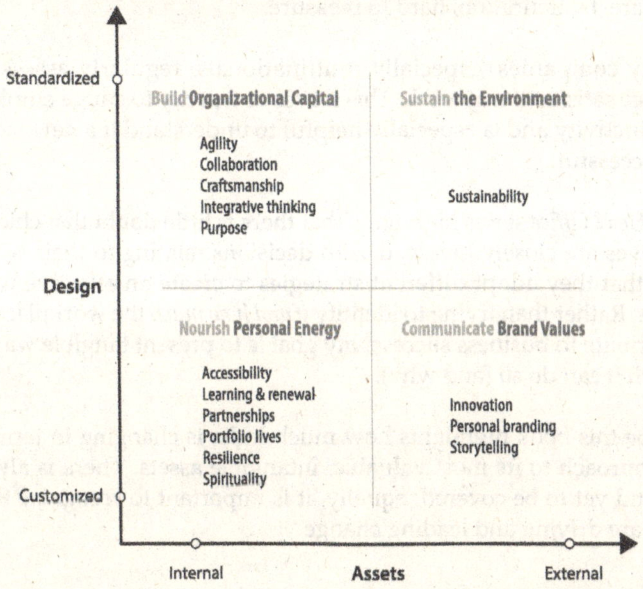

business leaders worked. I identified **'fifteen work styles'**, based on my observations of how CEOs managed the four intangible assets mentioned above–and used workplace design to do so. Each of these is validated by business management literature, as well as by current international research on workspaces.

Each business leader has thus been categorized into one of these fifteen work styles, based on what I felt was the best fit–i.e. the way of working that sets him or her apart from others. Please note that these classifications are not exhaustive or exclusive. Each individual exhibits more than one working style, of course, but has been classified based on the particular way of working that differentiates him or her from others.

These work styles tell us what progressive chief executives are like when they're at work, and how spaces have been configured to reinforce their ways of working. Each of these ways of working–and their corresponding leadership traits–is discussed in more detail later.

I am usually asked one question in particular, so I would like to take the liberty of pre-empting it:

What is the business impact of an effective workplace? There is no short answer, unfortunately, since workplaces impact intangible assets that are, by definition, hard to measure.

Many companies, especially multinationals, regularly assess employee satisfaction at work. This serves as a proxy to gauge employee productivity and is especially helpful to understand if a new facility is successful.

The *Head Office* series highlights that there is little doubt that chief executives are closely involved with decisions relating to their spaces, and that they adopt different strategies to create an effective workplace. Rather than trying to identify *if and how much* the workplace can contribute to business success, my goal is to present tangible ways in which it can do so (and why).

I hope this book highlights how much India is changing in terms of its approach to its most valuable, intangible assets. There is always ground yet to be covered, equally, it is important to recognize those who are driving and leading change.

HOW THIS BOOK WORKS

This book is divided into four sections, based on each type of intangible asset:

- Section I: Personal energy
- Section II: Organizational capital
- Section III: Brand values
- Section IV: Environment & sustainability

Within each of these four sections, there are specific work styles, and case studies to highlight best practice in each work style.

If you're interested in reading more about a particular individual or organization: The table of contents has the entire listing of forty chief executives and organizations, if you would like to locate anyone in particular. Each individual has been categorized based on his or her primary work style.

If you would like to know more about leadership and management: The book lists fifteen work styles, each of which forms the basis for specific leadership traits. A short note at the beginning of each chapter talks more about the connections between work styles, leadership traits and management thinking.

There is also a summary of the fifteen work styles (overleaf), which is intended to serve as a template to evaluate your way of working, and the kind of work environment you might find most productive.

If you are interested in knowing more about workplace design: The introductory note at the beginning of each of the four sections talks about the role of workplaces–whether they nourish personal energy, build organizational capital, communicate brand values or sustain the environment. There are also design triggers listed at the end of each section, to establish the connection between intangible assets and workplace design, and also to help design practitioners and business leaders to be more aligned.

WORK STYLE TEMPLATE

To help you assess your preferred work style and workplace archetype.

For each work style, there are two to four case studies that capture relevant best practice.

SECTION I: NOURISH PERSONAL ENERGY

Accessibility	*If you need to meet many people, have you set up systems to make it easy for people to connect with you, whether in person or tech-enabled?*
Learning & renewal	*Do you like to nourish your personal energy through books, music or nature?*
Partnerships	*Do you like working alongside a business partner?*
Portfolio lives	*Do you live a 'portfolio' life with a collection of many activities, rather than one full-time job?*
Resilience	*Would you consider yourself as being resilient to external change and focused on long-term institution building?*
Spirituality	*Do you refer to spiritual texts to help you navigate business life?*

SECTION II: BUILD ORGANIZATIONAL CAPITAL

Agility *Are you comfortable working in a flexible seating environment?*

Collaboration *Do you like working in an open-plan environment?*

Craftsmanship *How focused are you on product development? Do you think of your workplace as a studio for product development?*

Integrative thinking *Do you think of yourself as a 'smart creative' integrating both creativity and commerce?*

Purpose *Are you aligning your workplace and organization around a set of stated goals or a corporate misson?*

SECTION III: COMMUNICATE BRAND VALUES

Innovation *Do you believe workspaces should ignite and foster innovative thinking?*

Personal branding *Do you like to customize your workplace to express personal values and beliefs?*

Storytelling *Do you like your workspaces to tell a story about the company brand? Is the organization aligned around brand values?*

SECTION IV: SUSTAIN THE ENVIRONMENT

Sustainability *Do you believe in implementing sustainability goals as part of your corporate mission?*

Are you aligning your organizations and workspace around sustainable practices?

SECTION I: PERSONAL ENERGY

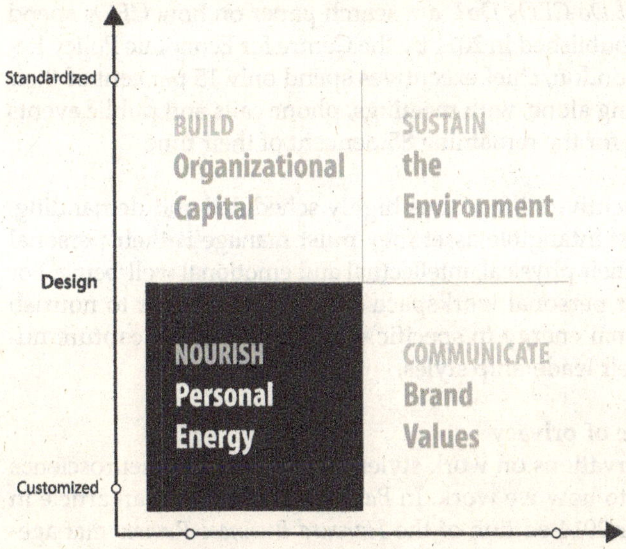

ANCHOR TO NOURISH PERSONAL ENERGY

The corner office is a universal symbol of power.

An enclosed space with a large desk, a high-backed chair, a sofa, a coffee table, a good view and at least one assistant seated outside in close proximity; these are key elements of the classic C-suite, anywhere in the world. It was unsurprising to note that most chief executives I met in the *Head Office* series chose to work out of such a space, albeit with varying degrees of transparency.

While the corner office represents corporate aspiration, it is also sometimes a source of mystery to junior corporate executives, who speculate about their boss' intentions or actions. *Head Office* tries to demystify some of the intrigue surrounding business leaders and their personal workspaces. During the course of my interviews with chief executives, I discovered what their private office meant to them, how they used it, and how it reflected their varied work styles.

Inner space

Most chief executives spend very little time on their own. According to *What Do CEOs Do?*, a research paper on how CEOs spend their time, published in 2011 by the Centre for Economic Policy Research in London, chief executives spend only 15 per cent of their time working alone, with meetings, phone calls and public events accounting for the remaining 85 per cent of their time.

A chief executive's life is thus highly scheduled and demanding, and the first intangible asset they must manage is their personal energy, or their physical, intellectual and emotional well-being. For many, their personal workspace serves as an anchor to nourish their personal energy in specific work styles, which capture nuances of their leadership styles.

The science of privacy

These observations on work styles are validated by neuroscience research into how we work. In *Balancing We and Me*, an article in the October 2014 edition of the *Harvard Business Review* management journal, researchers from Steelcase, one of the world's largest office furniture companies, outline the link between workspaces and neuroscience.

Neuroscience research identifies three basic modes of attention, they write. First, controlled attention, or working on a task that requires intense focus. Second, stimulus-driven attention–switching focus when something catches our attention, for example, interruptions when doing routine tasks. Finally, rejuvenation, or periodic respites from concentration during the day. 'The challenge is to find the right balance of social and private (space) and to provide spaces that enhance all modes,' they conclude.

Private offices such as C-suites allow occupants to easily switch between the three modes of attention, as their design facilitates both individual and interactive work. More importantly, an enclosed space allows occupants to control the amount of incoming stimulation (noise or distraction), when they're moving from one mode to another mode; being able to simply shut the door if it's too noisy outside, for example.

My research suggests that chief executives leverage their C-suites to nourish their personal energy through six different work styles. Some use their workspace as a tool to remain **accessible** to their stakeholders, while for others it is a site of **learning and renewal**. Those who lead a **portfolio life** find it a helpful anchor to balance their varied activities, and others, who operate as a **partnership**, have customized it to accommodate their specific way of working with their partners. Lastly, the C-suite can be tailored to suit different expressions of emotional intelligence, such as **resilience** and **spirituality**.

DESIGN TRIGGERS FOR A 'NOURISHING' WORKPLACE:

1. *Would you like to work alone or with someone?*
2. *How private or open would you like your space to be?*
3. *Would you like to meet people in your cabin or somewhere else?*
4. *Do you prefer coffee tables or discussion tables for meetings?*
5. *Would you like to videoconference as a regular form of communication?*
6. *What sort of artwork or decor do you find most nourishing?*
7. *Will you play music?*
8. *Do you read a lot?*

ACCESSIBILITY

Management thinker Peter Drucker, in his classic 2004 *Harvard Business Review* article, *What makes an effective executive?* writes 'executives must take responsibility for communicating' and 'organizations are held together by information rather than by ownership or command'.

Two chief executives who exemplify this trait are Deepak Parekh, chairman of Housing Development Finance Corporation, the nation's leading housing finance provider, and Natarajan Chandrasekaran, CEO of Tata Consultancy Services, India's most valuable private sector company by market capitalization.

Arguably two of the busiest members of the Indian corporate landscape, they are exceptional for their reach; for the number of people they are in touch with on a daily basis. Yet they are both highly accessible people, in the sense that they derive personal energy from meeting people, and have developed their own systems to allow the wider world to connect with them, share information and meet them, despite their busy schedules.

Yet their methods could not be more different. Parekh has a trio of assistants to filter emails and calls, an amazing memory and a completely outdated Nokia phone. Chandrasekaran is extremely technology-driven, and juggles various devices, but he is skilled at employing technology so that he is not at its mercy.

Their personal workplaces support this people-led way of working, by providing the right kind of infrastructure–whether support staff or technology–to allow them to remain accessible to all their stakeholders, without compromising on their individual privacy when needed.

Deepak Parekh's cabin overflows with literature of all kinds

DEEPAK PAREKH

THE FRIENDLY STATESMAN

It is 11.00 a.m. on a weekday morning and the *durbar* of Deepak Parekh is in full swing. Parekh is the chairman, Housing Development Finance Corp. (HDFC), and a veteran of the banking community; he is also an adviser and active committee member of various public, private and non-profit organizations.

His modest suite of rooms consists of cabins for him and his senior colleagues, workstations for supporting staff members, a waiting area and a boardroom, all with their doors left wide open. It is a textbook open office, not an intimidating 'corridor of power'. Located in HDFC's corporate office in Mumbai's downtown Churchgate, Parekh says his preferred format of a basic corner office 'hasn't changed in thirty-three years'.

The black Ganesha gifted by his wife thirty-three years ago when he joined HDFC

He moves from his personal cabin to the conference room, via a colleague's empty office, meeting visitors and responding to calls–assiduously, efficiently, continually. A trio of assistants, seated outside his cabin, reply to a battery of requests to meet or speak with him–

'We were set up in an age when things were different. There was more governance; the atmosphere in the outside world also was cleaner. Frugality was a virtue. Consumption was not at the centre.'

approximately 300 people, I am told, reach out to him daily. His work philosophy is as straightforward and unassuming as the workplace's wooden furniture: 'Meet anyone who wants to meet you.' Colleagues confirm that 'not a single mail, letter or call to him goes unanswered'.

Parekh is an old family friend, but this is our first meeting in a professional context. The encounter is enlightening–his workspace offers insight into the personality of a man often termed 'Mr Fixit' by the media for his troubleshooting abilities. The office reflects HDFC's spartan approach to spaces; functional, well-maintained furniture, limited artwork, some greenery. Apart from its simplicity, there are four pieces of office paraphernalia, in particular, which catch my attention.

Creating personal currency

First, a miniature yellow signboard, the kind one sees at accident sites, with the word 'compliance' and a sketch of a slippery slope, sits on his desk. It is a witty visual illustration of 'clean business'; a reminder of the importance of integrity in everyday life, and a metaphor for Parekh's personal currency of sound values. Parekh makes it a point to give it to executives of companies he is associated with as non-executive chairman, such as Siemens India.

The signboard on Parekh's desk

'We were set up in an age when things were different. There was more governance; the atmosphere in the outside world also was cleaner. Frugality was a virtue. Consumption was not at the centre,' explains Parekh, underlining the role of integrity in a financial institution with cash as its raw material. He adds: 'You can't manufacture culture. Culture builds in an organization over a period of time. And the tone at the top must be integrity, value systems.'

The boardroom

Second, books and papers dominate every possible surface, some neatly arranged in a circular-shaped formation on a coffee table. Much of this literature is complimentary (this includes the Kingfisher annual calendar).

The profusion of books, brochures and documents on a variety of subjects captures another vital ingredient of Parekh's professional success: his ability to engage with, absorb, retain and assimilate vast amounts of information, whether the subject matter is infrastructure, real estate, financial services or education.

'Honestly you need a separate life to read all the books you have,' he says. 'Meeting people,' he adds, 'gives you more information than anything else.'

Parekh says he gleans a lot of information from 'newspapers, television, magazines', and is categorical that he does not rely on books. 'Honestly you need a separate life to read all the books you have,' he says. 'Meeting people,' he adds, 'gives you more information than anything else.'

The third notable item is an outdated Nokia mobile phone, one of the oldest models available, which Parekh likes for its 'familiarity'. He recently started using an iPad, but in general eschews most modern computing equipment, relying instead on his memory to process information. 'You need to have an active mind', he

His three assistants manage multiple requests to meet him

reiterates. The card game Bridge is a favourite pursuit to improve retention skills, as is discipline: I learn that he makes it a point to 'do one five-star Sudoku every night, even if it is 12.00 at night, without writing, rubbing and erasing', to preserve mental agility.

Institutional loyalty

'You can't manufacture culture. Culture builds in an organization over a period of time. And the tone at the top must be integrity, value systems.'

Finally, there is a black Ganesha statue, prominently placed on a cabinet behind his desk, given by his wife Smita on his first day at HDFC. Thirty-three years later, it bears testimony to his institutional loyalty. Ask him what advice he would give a youngster, and his answer is unequivocal: 'patience'. Accumulated wisdom and consistent hard work deliver greater long-term benefits, he believes, than rapid job-hopping.

Parekh's work style–with its emphasis on old-fashioned virtues such as loyalty, credibility, transparency, willingness to aid and listen, reliance on one's memory over technology, the power of enduring relationships–might seem incongruous in the new century's frenzied workplace. Yet his unique position in India's business landscape underlines their relevance.

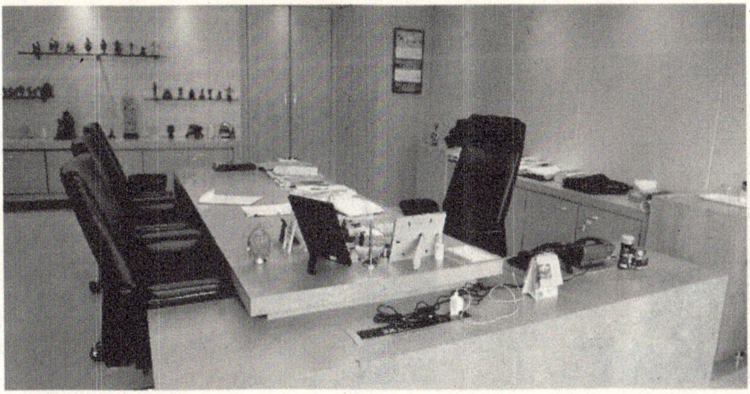

Parekh's new office retains the former workplace's simplicity and accessibility

I'd like to describe him as a 'friendly statesman' because I believe 'Mr Fixit' undermines his abilities: In my view, Parekh ranks as high as any of the country's longest-serving politicians. His constituency is vast, his stakeholders unlimited. Unlike most politicians, he's stayed in office for consecutive decades, and his sphere of influence has grown. It will be interesting to see who inherits his mantle–but hopefully, that day is a long way away.

22 April 2012

UPDATE: *HDFC moved into a new office in January 2014, in the same neighbourhood as before. Parekh continues to move between meetings, from boardroom to his cabin to other meeting rooms.*

NATARAJAN CHANDRASEKARAN

Chandrasekaran's spacious office has several cabinets full of official and personal memorabilia

THE CONVERSATIONAL TECHNOLOGIST

It is not often that I meet a chief executive who has 'outgrown' his C-suite, but this appears to be the case with Natarajan Chandrasekaran, whose workspace does not seem to entirely capture his business outlook or personality. Popularly known as 'Chandra', the chief executive of Tata Consultancy Services (TCS) runs India's largest IT services business, and also India's biggest company by market capitalization, currently valued at over ₹ 5,00,000 crores. Chandrasekaran's C-suite was the first to be featured in *Head Office* just over five years ago, in March 2010, a few months after he had officially taken over as CEO. I'm back to see if his workplace and work style have evolved.

Football signed by Pele

Room for change

As before, the spacious cabin continues to house a presidential desk, a large TV for videoconferencing and a coffee table surrounded by comfortable seating. The only significant change is that a round discussion table has been replaced by two storage units, displaying Chandrasekaran's books, official awards and an extensive collection of personal memorabilia.

Objects include mementoes from TCS offices and customers around the world, signed copies of sporting goods by world champions such as footballer Pele and tennis player Martina Navratilova, a portrait of Gandhi and one of long-distance runner John A. Kelley, both of which are 'a source of inspiration', says Chandrasekaran, a keen marathoner himself, who specifies, 'I'm fitter now than I was five years ago. My marathon time has come down to just under five hours.'

'I'm fitter now than I was five years ago. My marathon time has come down to just under five hours.'

Last time I visited, Chandrasekaran had surprised me with his early adoption of contemporary workplace practices, including remote working (one of his assistants worked from her home in a different city when we met) and habitual videoconferencing (at least one or two in a day was his common practice).

Five years later, he continues to be ahead of the curve: he has just started wearing an Apple watch ('the health apps are excellent'), he is investing heavily in design and innovation as a driver of customer-centricity for the business, and he wants to create agile workplaces, with flexible, rather than assigned seating, and more varied work settings.

'The whole industry is moving towards agile working. We've done it in our facilities in Pune, Chennai (in India), and Santa Clara, (in the US), and I want to do it in the corporate office (in Mumbai). Even on this floor, I would like to take out these walls, these partitions, have some completely informal [work] settings, as well as some formal seating. Perhaps have a high table where people can come and work,' he explains.

'What's happening, even for me, is that I have different ways of working. Sometimes I'm comfortable seated there (points to his desk), sometimes

Chandrasekaran videoconferences using a well-positioned, large TV screen

looking at a spreadsheet, thinking through a PowerPoint or emailing, writing a document. Sometimes, when I'm thinking through my problem, my normal style is to walk up and down. We have to create an environment like that,' he says. This is clearly a radically different outlook from his current workplace, which is an enclosed, private office, very traditional in its look and feel, as well as its functionality.

'The whole industry is moving towards agile working. We've done it in our facilities in Pune, Chennai (in India), and Santa Clara (in the US), and I want to do it in the corporate office (in Mumbai)'.

Process and outcome

Chandrasekaran is generally regarded as one of corporate India's most successful business leaders. Under his watch, TCS has more than tripled revenues (to ₹ 94,648 crores as of March 2015), and doubled its headcount (to over 3,00,000 employees) in the five years since he took over as its chief executive. So apart from understanding how his workplace has evolved, I am keen to understand his work style and specifically, how he manages his personal time and energy.

One of the answers, it turns out, rests in a trademark Chandrasekaran technique that I term as the 'right-tech-right-time' approach, or utilizing technology in an optimal way to communicate efficiently and productively, with as many stakeholders as possible.

First, email. Chandrasekaran has condensed email management into an art form. 'Five years ago, I undertook the exercise of looking at many of the emails I was getting. Now I get very few, about forty a day, of which about ten to fifteen are spam emails. The remaining emails are mostly for my information. I have to give guidance or a response to less than ten of them. That is because most of the decisions of running the business are with the next level,' he says, adding that face-to-face reviews, in person or over videoconferencing are far more effective than sending or receiving emails.

'Five years ago, I undertook the exercise of looking at many of the emails I was getting. Now I get very few, about forty a day.'

Second, conference calls. Chandrasekaran has almost eliminated the conference call from his calendar, because he finds them inefficient and unproductive, as participants are often distracted and inattentive during the call. 'My conference calls are five-ten minutes, and they are few and far between. I like one-to-one conference calls, or maybe a maximum of two or three people. Having a large group doesn't work for me,' he emphasizes.

Instead, he continues to rely heavily on videoconferencing. 'Structured videoconferences are very effective, if they have an agenda,' he says, citing that he regularly conducts monthly reviews, customer meetings or board meetings over videoconference, from either his personal workspace, a larger meeting room in the office or from his home office, depending on meeting size, time and duration.

Most importantly, Chandrasekaran is adept at adapting his work style to suit the person who he is interacting with. 'If you take my direct reports, some are very comfortable on SMS, some on phone calls, some on emails. It varies. It depends on the nature of the person, and also depends on

Plaque dedicated to famous marathoner Kelley

'Structured videoconferences are very effective, if they have an agenda.'

the situation. If someone takes a larger responsibility, till such time that they are comfortable, then they need to connect frequently. If someone is settled in the job, then they don't feel the need to connect as much. It's all about balance, and you don't follow the same approach with everyone,' he explains.

Perhaps it is this leadership trait that underlines Chandrasekaran's approach to communication and technology, and makes him so effective in managing his personal energy: outline the process, remain focused on the outcome and also allow for some element of personalization, and customize to make the process itself most effective. I wonder how long it will take for him to apply this outcome-oriented process to the corporate office redesign.

Gift from TCS office in Mexico

1 July 2015

UPDATE: *This is an updated version of a story first published on 14 March 2010.*

LEARNING & RENEWAL

Business leaders need to look after their physical, emotional and intellectual well-being. Learning is a proven technique for self-renewal, and for some chief executives, lifelong learning is an integral aspect of their working lives and their personal development. Although corner offices have fewer and fewer books, some private offices continue to serve as libraries for books and as sanctuaries for solitary reflection.

Harsh Mariwala, chairman of consumer products company Marico, has an extensive collection of business management books, as well as a set of clothbound notebooks where he records his own thoughts. Anil Khandelwal, former chairman of Bank of Baroda, built a fully fledged home office for himself, after retirement, to house his collection of over 2000 books, as well as to give him a greater sense of purpose.

Private offices can nourish and renew in other ways, as seen in the late Captain Nair's generous C-suite, which serves as a gentleman's club for meetings, an archive of his accomplishments and a zen garden of serenity. The decision to invest in such an office reflects Nair's ability to leverage spatial resources to nourish his personal energy. Since he was able to shoot basketball hoops well into his ninth decade, his office prompts us into envisioning how we might design our spaces to be similarly nourishing.

ANIL KHANDELWAL

Khandelwal in his home office; and his wife Vandna

THE BANKER-TURNED-AUTHOR

Office workers usually daydream about the future as a utopia where they are unshackled from their workstations. Anil Khandelwal, a former chairman and managing director of Bank of Baroda, is precisely the opposite. Retirement can be 'professional widowhood, especially in the public sector', Khandelwal professes, joking that 'no one calls you any more'.

The Lifetime Achievement Award that Anil Khandelwal received from The Asian Banker, Singapore, the first Indian to receive it

From 2005-08, under Khandelwal's leadership, Bank of Baroda doubled its business and its profits, with significantly improved employee productivity, and Khandelwal earned a reputation as a public sector banking turnaround expert. Even before his retirement from one of India's largest public sector banks, Khandelwal had anticipated the potential hazards of post-retirement slowdown.

Over the past few years, he has leveraged his experiences to construct a 'portfolio' career of diverse activities. This includes writing his autobiography, *Dare to Lead*, which was published in 2011, writing a regular column in a human resources magazine, chairing a national government committee, mentoring younger banking colleagues and advising private sector companies as a consultant or board member.

'Retirement can be widowhood, especially in the public sector.'

Khandelwal designed a quintessentially 'official' work environment for himself at home, in a high-rise residential block in Mumbai's Worli neighbourhood, with the help of his wife Vandana, who offered both creative and practical inputs. The approximately 8x8 ft room is 'small, yet functional', he says, and was converted from a staff utility and storage room, situated at the entrance of the flat.

For most people, a home office often serves as a library or study for personal contemplation, reading or writing. Business meetings at home usually take place in a more casual lounge with a sofa and a coffee table. Khandelwal's home office is different–it is clearly modelled as a senior manager's cabin for work-related meetings, as well as a library and study. I am keen to understand his motivations for creating such a businesslike workspace in his home.

Professional avatar, private space

This space has all the usual symbols of corporate chiefdom: a high-backed leather chair, a desk, two chairs for visitors, a flat-screen television, computer equipment and several shelves of box files. A line of trophies is perched neatly atop a storage unit. Two wall mounted photo collages capture Khandelwal's professional accomplishments and family travels, and conceal the electrical fittings behind. A whiteboard lists his appointments for the day.

The only indications of the room's non-corporate location are its floor to ceiling bookshelves: Khan-

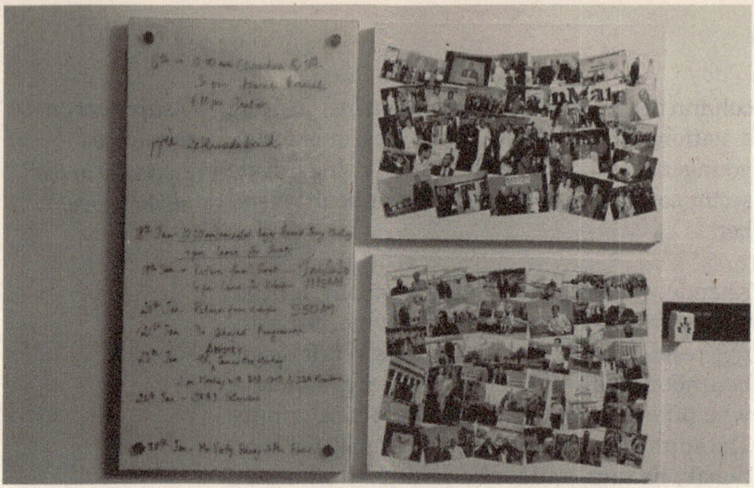

A marker board and a selection of family photographs

delwal says he has more than 2000 books, largely on management literature, which he describes as his 'treasure trove'. The collection spans business stalwarts such as Jack Welch and Jim Collins, as well as more unusual fare such as *Tempered Radicals* by Debra Meyerson and *Dialogue and the Art of Thinking Together* by William Isaacs–two of his favourites.

'The whole idea is that I am in an office, I don't have that psychological drain that I am not working. Maybe it gives me a surrogate sense of remaining a CEO.'

The home office is the venue for his meetings, phone conversations, writing and reading. 'The whole idea is that I am in an office, I don't have that psychological drain that I am not working. Maybe it gives me a surrogate sense of remaining a CEO,' he admits. He observes nine-to-five office hours, although he now takes exercise breaks during the day, and has recently learnt to swim.

Lessons for home office design

The design offers lessons to all those who work from home.

First, placement. Most of us camp at the dining table when working from home (Khandelwal says he did so himself while with the bank). This is neither ergonomically advisable, nor particularly convenient for other household members. By assigning a dedicated room at the entrance of the apartment for his personal study-library -office, Khandelwal says he manages to remain 'inside-out'–at home but not intruding on his wife's territory; she smiles in agreement. For others, if a separate room is not available, a quiet spot in the master bedroom (which is usually unoccupied during working hours) is preferable to taking over the family living room.

His autobiography describes his tenure as 'an exhilarating, life-changing three years' and an 'unforgettable' experience.

Second, functionality. For those who spend several hours at a stretch working from home, the home office must perform as well as a commercial interior fit-out. Lighting, ventilation, technology, furniture, computer equipment and storage are all important considerations in maximizing efficiency from a compact space.

Third, personalization. Home offices allow for much desired individual expression. Effective design, in terms of functionality as well as aesthetics and form, must hinge on the most important criteria for the occupant. The starting point for Khandelwal's home office was the need to neatly preserve and display his enviable library. His wife mentions that dedicated storage was critical to accommodate sprawling stacks of books. Other design factors could include taking advantage of a great view, preserving a prized antique desk, or fitting in technology.

Finally, it highlights the extent to which our personal and professional notions of identity are intertwined. 'If this room was not there, I don't know how miserable my life would have been,' Khandelwal confesses.

As his writings show, Khandelwal is certainly a consummate public sector banker. Despite the complex challenges faced by heads of public sector banks, his autobiography describes his tenure as 'an exhilarating, life-changing three years' and

Custom-made bookshelves accommodate his collection of over 2000 books, largely business management titles

an 'unforgettable' experience.

Given his full throttle endorsement of public sector life, it is unsurprising that he has established a corporate headquarters for himself in his personal domain. With longer working lives, 'portfolio' careers, and increasingly blurred boundaries between business and pleasure, our daily work–and our workplaces–can actually be a source of personal fulfillment, whether we care to admit this or not.

22 January 2012

Nair's multi-room suite at the Leela in Mumbai has distinct spaces for meetings, discussions, dining and resting.

CAPTAIN C.P. KRISHNAN NAIR

THE HOSPITABLE GARDENER

Seated before me is a company chairman who shoots basketball hoops before breakfast, wears black Nike trainers to work and answers my questions with a joyous chuckle. None of this betrays the fact that he is on the cusp of completing the ninth decade of his life.

I am in the 1228 sq. ft chairman's suite, on the eighth floor of the Leela Kempinski hotel in Mumbai. The apartment-sized suite is composed of two dedicated workspaces for the chairman and his assistant, a living room, a dining room and a bedroom. The suite's octogenarian occupant and titular head of the luxury hotel chain, Capt. C.P. Krishnan Nair, decided to have a suite for himself when the hotel was constructed in 1987. His daughter-in-law, Madhu Nair, was involved in the design of the suite since she is responsible for the interior design of group properties.

Photographs of Nair with national and international leaders

An array of idols line his shelves, including a Buddha statue personally gifted by the Dalai Lama

Inclusive workplace design

My encounter with Nair, who celebrated his eighty-ninth birthday earlier this month, is prompted by *Work Well: Inclusive Furniture for Older Office Workers*, a research report on 'inclusive' workplace design 'for older office workers'. Published in 2005 by the Helen Hamlyn Research Centre at the Royal College of Art (RCA) in London, one of the world's most respected design schools, its findings are increasingly gaining relevance.

His space simultaneously performs three roles; as a gentleman's club for elegant discourse, an archive of his accomplishments and a zen garden of serenity.

Working hours are swelling; retirement is often a moving target, and post-retirement careers prolong an office-based existence. The report investigated the suitability of modern workplaces for an ageing workforce (designated as those 'over fifty') and arrived at an uncomfortable truth: Workplaces are usually insensitive to the physical, mental and emotional needs of older workers. Shortcomings include usability problems in furniture and lighting, inadequate amenities for breaks during office hours, lack of spaces for knowledge sharing and increased health issues from working on the move.

The report was Europe-based, but its findings are universally applicable, even for a country such as

India, with its reputed 'demographic dividend' of a youthful population. Our enormous population translates into a sizeable senior workforce of 71 million people aged over sixty, according to the 2001 census–the second largest in the world. So I decide to visit the offices of one of India's most sprightly octogenarian business leaders.

'Plants can feel, they can hear, they can smell and they can live with you.'

Serene splendour

How important is work environment in extending individual shelf life? I wonder. An in-depth look at Nair's workplace suggests it certainly helps. His space simultaneously performs three roles. It is a gentleman's club for elegant discourse. It is an archive of his accomplishments over the decades. Finally, it is a zen garden of serenity. The roles reflect his personality and profession, and accommodate his needs as elder statesman.

In form and function, the five-room suite resembles a country club, with dedicated spaces for assorted tasks. Important meetings are held in a formal office, which has an assistant's cabin adjoining it. Architectural plans and marketing materials for new properties can be spread out and reviewed with colleagues on the six-seater dining table, on which Nair also has lunch every day. Informal conversations, such as our interview, take place in the living room. He retires to the bedroom for a short nap after lunch, a practice he began three years ago.

As an upmarket hotelier, Nair's remit is to entertain world leaders and celebrities, a duty he clearly relishes. Framed photographs with world leaders such as US President Barack Obama and the Dalai Lama, the Tibetan spiritual leader, line the shelves of his office, jostling for space with numerous industry awards and citations, transforming the hotel suite into a museum of his professional history. He shows me a recent curious

For all its lavish 'exclusivity', Nair's office meets every RCA report criterion for an 'inclusive' workplace.

letter from the maharaja of Kerala, asking Nair for a trained cook, and another from him to Obama, inviting him to visit the Leela properties.

Finally, the chairman's suite is a shrine to God and flora. 'I love to be in the company of gods, even though it's my workplace,' Nair says. Statues of Buddha and Ganesha adorn the mantelpiece and bookshelf. Each idol is decorated with a single flower, as poised as the trademark silk handkerchief peeping out from his blazer pocket.

Flowers have been a lifelong passion. 'Plants can feel, they can hear, they can smell and they can live with you,' he says. Adding, 'When (the) New Delhi (hotel in Chanakyapuri) opens I want to get the most exotic flowers from all across the world and decorate it.' Our conversation is punctuated with references to mangroves, tamarind, jasmine, laburnums and 'thirty varieties of plumeria–from Argentina, Rio de Janeiro, Hawaii, Malaysia, Singapore and Bangkok'.

It takes a suite

For all its lavish 'exclusivity', Nair's office meets every RCA report criterion for an 'inclusive' workplace. Its occupant has been able to personalize his space. Varied work settings facilitate individual and group work, allowing Nair to take necessary breaks. The presence of nature and divinity promote emotional well-being.

Nair cherishes his meeting with Gandhi decades ago, and has placed a print of Gandhi in his dining room

The nurturing work environment just happened, however. 'I have not related how it affects my life, my work, but I keep doing it unknowingly,' he says. Rather, the decision to invest in such an office reflects Nair's ability to align physical space with intellectual needs. Daily basketball sessions with his physiotherapist and the Nike New Balance walking shoes, adopted as daily attire fifteen years ago, are also examples of how he welds mind and body. The discipline he has retained from an initial stint in the army, sixty years of following the tenets of Ayurveda, and a cheerful disposition are even more critical drivers of his robust constitution.

The decision to invest in such an office reflects Nair's ability to align physical space with intellectual needs.

Nair is fortunate. As company chairman and hotel owner, he has the rare privilege of occupying an entire suite that caters to his specific needs. His office was designed when he was sixty-five, well into his senior years, so it is not surprising that the office space and its occupant are perfectly matched. Sons Vivek and Dinesh, both managing directors in the business, have more conventional offices located on the management floor.

But such a space is rare, and it only highlights how little modern workplaces do to accommodate the average ageing knowledge worker. Ironically, most office design and investment decisions are typically taken by senior management themselves. Must it take a chairman's suite to guarantee extended working hours?

20 February 2011

UPDATE: *Captain Nair passed away on 17 May 2014.*

HARSH MARIWALA

Mariwala's office has a study-like feel to it with his large writing desk against the wall

THE INSIDE-OUT THINKER

Harsh Mariwala, the chairman of consumer products company Marico Ltd, has a terrace garden and an exceptional view of Mumbai airport's landing strip. He can see planes taking off and landing. But what really differentiates the eighth-floor office in Mumbai's Kalina area is an increasingly rare set of objects in contemporary corporate offices: books. To be more specific, a library of books on business management and a stack of clothbound notebooks on a shelf above his desk.

While most chief executives have a handful of books in their office, very few have such an extensive collection that each book warrants a number label (the highest count I saw was No. 451). 'I read one book a month, on average. I read on weekends, on flights, in the car, on my bike in my gym, or when waiting for someone. I always have a book in my bag,' Mariwala says, adding, 'I had to give away over 200 books when I moved into this office last year because I was told there wasn't enough space.'

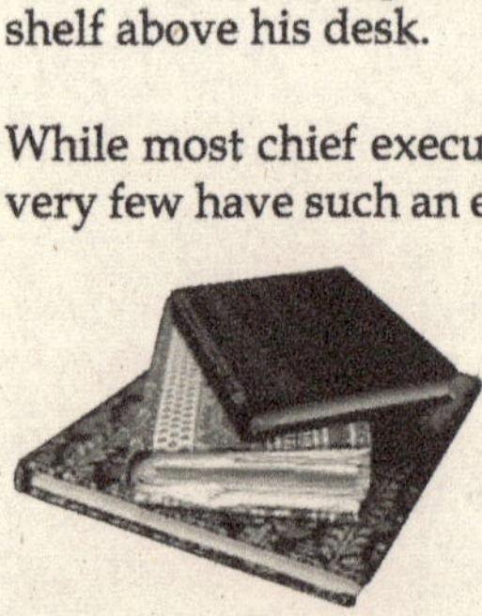

Clothbound notebooks with quotes and typed out summaries from Harsh Mariwala's favourite business books

The clothbound notebooks contain typed out summaries and quotes from books by his favourite business authors, which include C.K. Prahalad, Ram Charan and Raj Sisodia. Mariwala highlights select quotes in the books, and his assistant types and pastes them in a notebook–a refreshingly quaint practice in today's Kindle-ized world. He is also writing a business book, 'all by hand', based on his entrepreneurial experiences, which he hopes to complete in the next few months.

'I read one book a month, on average. I read on weekends, on flights, in the car, on my bike in my gym, or when waiting for someone. I always have a book in my bag.'

The office itself has a study-like feel to it, and was designed by his wife Archana and a team of architects when Marico decided to move its corporate headquarters from Bandra to Kalina.

With its white marble floors, contemporary artwork, a large writing desk, sofa and TV, the office is serene, comfortable and personalized, closer to a home office in look and feel. The writing table is placed against a wall, with a small meeting table next to it, a departure from a presidential-style desk. 'I didn't want any barriers between me and the other person,' says Mariwala.

Competing on culture

The collection of management books–with a particular skew towards culture, innovation and purpose–highlights two of Mariwala's defining traits: his interest in corporate culture as a source of competitive advantage, and his ability to reinvent himself as a business leader. It is no coincidence that the only other chief executive I've met with such an extensive library, Anil Khandelwal, was a former human resource professional, with a similar interest in the people side of a business.

A custom-made bookshelf accommodates his extensive collection

'Culture eats strategy for breakfast,' Mariwala

The spacious office looks out onto a terrace garden

believes, quoting management guru Peter Drucker. He applies this dictum through a business philosophy aimed at building an 'empowered organization, with a high degree of trust and a defined set of values'. This belief is expressed in several ways: Employee attendance is not recorded and they maintain their own leave cards. Training is important–for new recruits to learn company values, for senior leaders to become better coaches and for business associates, alongside company employees.

'We compete against multinationals and they have a lot of career options outside India. We have to do something unique and differentiated, and empowerment is part of that.'

The approach is strongly rooted in business pragmatism. 'We compete against multinationals and they have a lot of career options outside India. We have to do something unique and differentiated, and empowerment is part of that,' explains Mariwala.

Last month, Mariwala formally resigned as managing director, handing over management control to an experienced professional, Saugata Gupta–the most significant expression of his belief in 'empowered organizations'.

The move also captures his ability to reinvent himself, from entrepreneur and founder to business head and now, a guide and mentor. 'My objective is to go on adding value and influencing, rather than controlling. I read a lot, I interact a lot, I think a lot and I review everything with my team,' he says, describing his new role.

'The purpose of life is a life of purpose.'

It is important to be rational when handing over hands-on management control, he stresses. 'You should not be emotional, you should not say what is good for the family first. What is good for the company is good for the family. As the largest shareholder, you get the financial benefit,' he says. This is clear logic at a pivotal time for Marico as it transitions from a branded oils company to a multi-brand, consumer product firm, operating in the highly competitive categories of beauty and wellness.

Catalyst for innovation

Mariwala's work approach can be captured by a phrase he uses to describe Marico's approach to work: 'Inside-out' thinking or 'thinking which comes from within, from our values and who we are', says Mariwala (the opposite of 'outside-in' thinking, shaped primarily by the external environment).

Mariwala is changing his life from the 'inside-out', taking on new roles, based on his personal beliefs, values, skills and experiences. Among the many projects he looks at closely at the Marico Innovation Foundation, social entrepreneurs are spurred to greater heights through the Social Innovation Acceleration Programme, where they are given 'just ₹ 20 lakh a year', says Mariwala, and extensive hands-on support to help them scale up.

The books in his cabin, especially *Firms of Endearment: How World-Class Companies Profit from Passion and Purpose* by Sisodia, David B. Wolfe and Jagdish Sheth, serve as inspiration. 'The

An award for business excellence

purpose of life is a life of purpose,' he says, citing one of his favourite quotes. 'I want to have a catalytic role in innovation, to have greater impact, not by building infrastructure myself but by helping other innovators, especially social innovators, to scale up.'

7 April 2014

PARTNERSHIPS

Although the leadership role of an organization is usually assumed by a single individual, it was interesting to encounter several partnerships- whether husbands and wives, such as fellow lawyers Cyril and Vandana Shroff, philanthropic catalysts Deval Sanghavi and Neera Nundy-or colleagues Vysyaprath Sunil and Mohit Dhar Jayal from advertising agency Wieden+Kennedy.

Their spaces were clearly configured to suit individual ways of working: one couple sits at the same large desk, another sits facing each other, and the third are seated close to each other, all within arm's length.

This practice of co-location or working at close proximity is corroborated by management research into the effect of new technology on proximity. Researchers Ben Waber, Jennifer Magnolfi and Greg Lindsay, authors of *Workspaces That Move People*, an article in the October 2014 edition of the *Harvard Business Review*, observed in one study that engineers who share a physical office were 20 per cent more likely to stay in touch digitally than those who worked elsewhere. When they needed to collaborate closely, co-located co-workers emailed four times as frequently as colleagues in different locations, which led to 32 per cent faster project completion times. The article highlights an important conclusion 'that both face-to-face and digital communications follow the Allen curve'.

Thomas Allen, a management professor at the MIT Sloan School of Management, discovered an interesting relationship between people, communication and physical distances, which is now called the Allen Curve. In his groundbreaking book *Managing the Flow of Technology*, published in 1984, the researchers write that he concluded that 'we are four times as likely to communicate regularly with someone sitting six feet away as with someone seated sixty feet away, and that we almost always never communicate with colleagues on separate floors or in separate buildings'.

If the Allen curve holds true, despite the advent of new technology, then it is a clear indication that proximity cannot be ignored as a driver of productivity.

CYRIL & VANDANA SHROFF

Cyril shares a hefty L-shaped desk with his wife Vandana Shroff, also a trained lawyer as it 'enables a high degree of coordination'

THE 24/7 PARTNERS

I am at the office of legal eagle Cyril Shroff, the Mumbai-based managing partner of Amarchand & Mangaldas & Suresh A. Shroff and Co., and his glass-walled workspace is unusual in many respects.

The first oddity is the curious seating arrangement–Cyril shares a hefty L-shaped desk with his wife Vandana Shroff, also a trained lawyer. They are one of the few husband-and-wife combinations to share a private office in corporate India. Although Vandana has a dedicated office space next door, they find it more convenient for her to work at his desk. It enables 'a high-level of coordination', Cyril says, adding that his parents worked in a similar fashion for several years too.

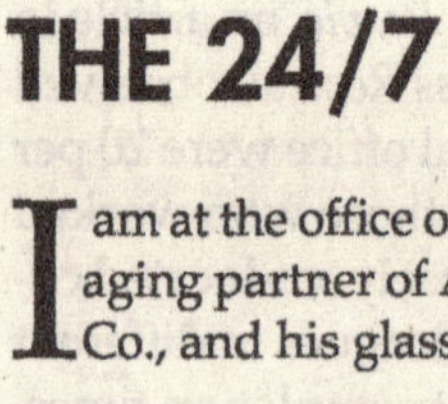

A pair of 150-year-old porcelain dogs

Second, Cyril appears to have a rather soft corner for dogs. A stuffed toy puppy sits beside a clutch of sharpened pencils on his desk. A pair of 150-year-old porcelain dogs rests on the cabinet unit. The family pug's snapshot serves as wallpaper on his mobile phone. Such sentimentality is somewhat incongruous with Cyril's reputedly razor-sharp legal acumen.

Traces of the Shroff family, past and present, punctuate the cabin and its immediate surroundings. A portrait of the late Suresh Shroff, Cyril's father, looms over the leather armchair next to Cyril and Vandana's desk. A similar portrait of Amarchand, Cyril's grandfather, hangs in the adjoining eight-seater meeting room where he meets larger groups of colleagues. Further down the corridor, a vacant cabin has several hand-drawn sketches by Cyril, depicting a range of subjects.

The old-world office decor conveys important firm values such as 'timelessness', 'continuity' and 'pedigree' to clients and employees, Cyril explains.

Next to the Shroffs' joint cabin is Vandana's 'lounge', an open meeting space, distinctively domestic in appearance with its luxurious armchairs, carpet and artefacts. A vibrant Jehangir Sabavala painting anchors the room. It is just one of an extensive collection of artwork sprinkled throughout the office, assiduously curated by Vandana. 'I look at art as an investment in my own happiness,' she says.

Traditional, yet contemporary

Cyril summarizes the office decor aesthetic in one word: *khandaani*. Vandana and he deliberately chose the old-school look, with teakwood furniture, leather armchairs and an extensive art collection, when they first bought the 25,000 sq. ft property spread over a floor and a half in Parel, and designed the office. It conveys important firm values such as 'timelessness', 'continuity' and 'pedigree' to clients and employees, Cyril explains.

Although old-fashioned in form, the workspace is contemporary in function, with modern-day computing technology, open-plan workstations and meeting rooms for firm-wide collaboration.

Amarchand was one of the first corporate entities to sense Mumbai's shifting axis of business and

Vandana's 'lounge', an open meeting space, has luxurious armchairs, carpet and artefacts

relocate from downtown Dalal Street to post-industrial Parel, nearly a decade ago. This marriage of traditional values with contemporary work practices highlights the benefits of having a promoter family in a professional services firm, believes Cyril. 'A founder's ability to take risks and provide entrepreneurship is significantly greater (than non-family professionals),' he states.

'A founder's ability to take risks and provide entrepreneurship is significantly greater (than non-family professionals).'

Unique business model

Three generations of Shroffs work in the 'family trade'–Cyril's mother, Bharati, the couple and their London-educated son Rishabh in Mumbai, and brother Shardul Shroff, his wife Pallavi and their children in Delhi. Cyril's daughter Paridhi is currently at law school.

Founded in 1917, Amarchand continues to dominate legal rankings in India in headcount (nearly 550 lawyers across five cities) and blue-chip corporate clientele. I am keen to understand how the dynamics of a firm such as this–structured as a partnership and led by a family–are reflected in its workplace.

The design, layout and contents of the workspace reinforce my perception of Amarchand as having a unique business model in the Indian corporate landscape. It is a family-led and family-managed, yet extremely successful professional services firm–an arrangement that might seem to be a contradiction in terms.

'Our leadership doesn't come from shareholding, it comes from intellectual leadership. The founder family (in a professional service firm) must provide financial capital, relationship capital and knowledge capital.'

Outsiders might question whether the presence of family members implies that the firm is not professionally run. For an expert opinion, I consulted Tom DeLong, one of my professors at Harvard Business School, and author of several books, articles and case studies on professional service firms.

Speaking over the phone, DeLong told me that Amarchand's organization structure has few global precedents. Citing the future entry of foreign law firms into India, he cautions that 'it will be more and more of a challenge, going forward, to combine family-owned business and the practice of law', as both clients and human talent might prefer to work for multinational law firms.

Cyril acknowledges that Amarchand has 'a challenging model; because if you look at it from the non-family professional's perspective, they may wonder whether this means anything less than a meritocracy'. But he also stresses that 'our leadership doesn't come from shareholding, it comes from intellectual leadership'. The founder family, in a professional service firm, must provide 'financial capital, relationship capital and knowledge capital', he emphasizes.

The Shroffs' workplace, and Amarchand's organization structure, neatly exemplify my belief that the 'family trade' (as seen in any sphere of life, whether business, politics or the arts) is still considered a solid Indian institution. Unlike other parts of the world, a decades-old family name in India connotes trust and reliability, rather than nepotism, giving it legitimacy.

A stuffed toy puppy

Several hand-drawn sketches by Cyril Shroff line the walls at the office

The Shroffs' office is thus an excellent barometer of Indian corporate zeitgeist when it comes to contemporary workplace culture. It captures our ability to modernize, while maintaining centuries-old tradition. Switch to iPads, install flat-screen monitors and laptops, but don't forget to ensure that the founder's portrait is prominently displayed.

8 May 2011

UPDATE: *AMSS was officially dissolved on 9 May 2015, after several months of mediation between Cyril and Shardul Shroff. Cyril's new firm, which was launched on 11 May 2015, is called Cyril Amarchand Mangaldas; his brother's new firm, called Shardul Amarchand Mangaldas, was launched on 10 May 2015.*

Nundy and Sanghavi choose to work on desks facing each other, alongside their senior team

NEERA NUNDY & DEVAL SANGHAVI

THE SOCIAL MULTIPLIERS

Neera Nundy and Deval Sanghavi, partners and co-founders of Dasra, a non-profit which connects corporate philanthropists with non-governmental organizations (NGOs), work out of what I would call a 'hybrid workspace'.

The Dasra office is part of a residential building in a quiet lane in Mumbai's Santa Cruz. Nundy and Sanghavi's room, at the top of the building, resembles an entry-level management consultant's office–a few colleagues seated in a room which has little other than several laptops. Office decor consists mostly of paintings gifted by non-profits and official citations.

Nundy's MBA degree from Harvard University, US

Nundy and Sanghavi, a married couple, sit facing each other; their executive leadership team of three professionals takes up the rest of the room. This uncommon arrangement was by design. 'We were keen to build a senior management team as a cohesive group which is enabled by sitting together in an open room. The close proximity allows you to help each other quickly,

'The close proximity allows you to help each other quickly, without the formalities of email or setting up meetings–and it's fun.'

without the formalities of email or setting up meetings–and it's fun,' says Nundy.

Elsewhere, teams of young professionals huddle over computers in open-plan workstations and a conference room. There's even corporate signage for different departments, located across three floors of the building. Only minor quirks, such as a tree that unexpectedly cuts through the ceiling of a conference room downstairs, suggest that this workplace is somewhat unconventional–neither a residential start-up nor a corporate office, but a hybrid space.

Platforms for giving

One of Dasra's biggest achievements is its Giving Circle–a platform that enables wealthy philanthropists to collectively donate their money to NGOs in a targeted and strategic manner. Individual donors commit to giving ₹ 10 lakh a year for three consecutive years to a particular sector or cause, such as adolescent girls or livelihoods. Ten individual donors are grouped into one Giving Circle, resulting in ₹ 1 crore annually for three years, to be allocated to an NGO chosen by the donors.

Dasra produces research reports on various sectors throughout the year, outlining the most effective NGOs in that space. 'For each of our reports, we look at 300 organizations to nominate the top three or ten, for example, that make most impact,' says Sanghavi. Giving Circle donors then vote to choose one of these NGOs for fund allocation. They can also volunteer their time, skills or networks to help the chosen NGO to scale up. To date, Dasra has directed ₹ 21 crores via seven Giving Circles, engaging eighty-five philanthropists.

The reports also have a multiplier effect on the sector. 'Our reports are now being downloaded

A tree cuts through a work area at Dasra

off our website by government, by funders, by researchers, raising tremendous awareness for the sector,' says Sanghavi. The organization's annual philanthropy forum has grown into a three-day conference–this year's edition, held last week, was attended by 600 people, with varied interests in the social sectors.

Managing hybrids

So how does one successfully build a hybrid platform, bridging two different communities? Nundy and Sanghavi's workplace offers some clues.

'For each of our reports, we look at 300 organizations to nominate the top three or ten, for example, that make most impact.'

First, work out how best to amalgamate diverse environments. Their workspace has the warmth of a home with the structure of a corporate office–with sixty-five people, it is more organized than the average residential start-up, yet less efficient than a large, open-plan office.

Both Sanghavi and Nundy were educated in the West, and worked at investment bank Morgan Stanley before starting Dasra in 1999. Business terms such as fund-raising, portfolio management, strategic planning, balanced scorecards and investor communication are as much part of Dasra's daily vocabulary as traditional non-profit

A drawing and poster from Dasra-supported non-profits

concerns such as malnutrition, sanitation and empowerment of adolescent girls in rural areas.

The hybrid model entails finding innovative solutions to address stakeholders' differing viewpoints, for example, with respect to time. Social impact begins with behavioural change, which takes time. 'Giving a toilet to a person does not guarantee they'll use it. It takes three-five years to convince individuals who have defecated a certain way to do it differently,' says Sanghavi.

'Donors like the leverage effect–I'm actually giving ₹ 10 lakh but I'm getting reported back over a crore.'

But corporate philanthropists are accustomed to faster results. So the Giving Circle model addresses this gap in timelines by asking donors to stay committed for enough time to bring change, and then delivering the multiplier effect of a group investment. 'They like the leverage effect–I'm actually giving ₹ 10 lakh but I'm getting reported back over a crore,' says Nundy.

Second, evolve continuously. Both Dasra's business model and its workspaces have adapted to the outside environment in the past decade. Nundy and Sanghavi first operated from their two-bedroom flat in Kandivali, juggling work and babysitting their three boys.

Family and team photographs

The couple started off running training programmes for non-profits. 'It took us ten years to learn from the market, to make mistakes, to really create a model that was sustainable before we actually hit the market,' says Sanghavi. 'A big learning for us was that providing capital without a significant amount of managerial support, or just managerial support without money, is detrimental. Just like any private equity investments,' explains Nundy.

'It took us ten years to learn from the market, to make mistakes, to really create a model that was sustainable before we actually hit the market.'

They later shifted their office out of their home to increasingly larger spaces, based on affordability and need. The tree in the conference room illustrates their adaptive attitude: They needed more space, but didn't want to cut it down, so they built a room around it.

Finally, specialize, but continuously collaborate. Nundy manages internal operations, while Sanghavi handles external responsibilities, but by being co-located at work, not separated by partitions, it's easier to stay connected.

Sound lessons, for a business world increasingly driven by platforms and complicated by diversity.

9 March 2014

VYSYAPRATH SUNIL & MOHIT DHAR JAYAL

The sunlit conference room is set apart from the main workspace

THE BRAND EVANGELISTS

The *Head Office* column occasionally serves as a reminder of how people and workplaces can remain consistent, despite changing circumstances. For example, the Delhi office of Vysyaprath Sunil and Mohit Dhar Jayal, the duo leading the Indian arm of global advertising agency Wieden+Kennedy, as executive creative director and director, respectively. The partnership is best known for its work on 'Make In India', the central government's flagship campaign to boost manufacturing, as well as on low-cost airline IndiGo and motorcycle manufacturer Royal Enfield.

A cargo ship installation by Prasad Raghavan

When I first met them in mid-2012, they had turned the most unexpected location–a former wedding hall on the lower ground floor of a Delhi Development Authority office block in Sheikh Sarai, south Delhi–into a creative, edgy workplace, with contemporary installation art, subtle lighting and open-plan desks.

Having moved offices in late 2012, I find them again located in an equally unusual destination: on the second floor of the DLF South Court shopping mall, adjacent to the popular Select Citywalk mall in Saket. 'We didn't want to be in Gurgaon like everyone else and we thought that we could get close to our (client's) consumers. Select Citywalk is one of India's busiest malls,' says Sunil.

'We didn't want to be in Gurgaon like everyone else and we thought that we could get close to our (client's) consumers.'

Creative interiors

The unconventional workspace is split into two–a larger office space, where the workstations, library and a few meeting rooms are located, and then another suite of meeting spaces, including a large sunlit conference room, situated further along the corridor and physically disconnected from the main workspace, in a quiet, almost isolated part of the mall. Sunil says they really liked 'this kind of glass box in the middle of nowhere', and judging from the quality of late afternoon light illuminating the space, its appeal is easy to understand.

The installation art has kept pace with relocation. An installation of 30,000 pencils, with the message 'Work is Workship' and a red rocking horse continue to be placed at the reception. Inside, there are several new pieces of contemporary art, including a wooden foot by Riyas Komu and a prominent cargo ship by Prasad Raghavan.

Some works are left over from the gallery that the duo used to run, which they closed down as they felt it was a conflict of interest with Sunil's involvement with the Kochi-Muziris Biennale, as joint secretary of the board of trustees of the international contemporary art exhibition held in Kochi. 'We thought that we could not be part of the Biennale and also run the commercial gallery. And also we don't want to have the responsibility of galleries, storage and worrying about artists and all that,' says Sunil.

Jayal and Sunil work at open-plan desks alongside colleagues

'For us, brand strategy is formed around a creative point of view or a brand voice or an editorial voice. So we always discuss where we think the brand is going to go between us.'

Fluid partnerships

Their physical working relationship has also evolved. Previously, Sunil and Jayal sat facing each other in adjacent glass cabins. Now, the cabins have gone and they sit alongside their colleagues, on separate open-plan desks, close to each other, but not separated by a partition.

It is a major change, especially considering that their cabins were filled with personal objects and artefacts. The more fluid set-up occurred partly by necessity ('we needed cabin space for meetings,' says Jayal), and partly by design. 'I always sit outside in any case (with the creative team) and I realized actually how all the things in my room, I don't actually need them,' says Sunil. 'Possessions are meaningless,' echoes Jayal, saying that both took a few important objects home and got rid of the rest.

Their decision to unshackle themselves from their cabins highlights another aspect of contemporary working life–little work actually gets done in cabins these days, and much more time is spent meeting colleagues and clients, either formally in meeting rooms, or informally, in collaboration spaces or even just at other team members' desks.

Many agencies operate with a partnership at the top, between the creative head and the account management head. Yet, Jayal and Sunil's work style is interesting because their partnership goes further, in three ways.

'Our core skill now is partnership. We make good partners. We identify people whose sensibilities we share, who are really creative at what they do.'

As I'd noticed the first time I met them, the roles are less divisible into creative and account management. 'For us, brand strategy is formed around a creative point of view or a brand voice or an editorial voice. So we always discuss where we think the brand is going to go between us. Because it's us talking, often the creative just tumbles straight out and it's perfect,' described Jayal when I first met them.

Second, Sunil and Jayal continue to work closely with their clients, with the client allowing the creative agency a much wider remit, than just communications. For example, in the case of IndiGo, Sunil, Jayal and their team got involved with operational aspects of the brand such as food tastings and airline interior design. 'Not everybody's equipped to handle (this level of proximity),' admits Jayal. 'I think we're strongly opinionated about it and it takes someone who really connects with us to smoothly take that on board and then make it a part of their process.'

Most recently, the agency has partnered with the Department of Industrial Policy and Promotion (DIPP) to create the 'Make In India' campaign, which Jayal describes as 'an unusually intense collaboration'. Sunil agrees, 'It's deadly. Work is happening in a super high-tech way. You don't even think it's like a government project. It is something else altogether.'

A wooden red rocking horse at the reception

Finally, the duo are taking their partnership further, to ally with strategic investors in non-advertising-related projects, relating to real estate

'What we can do is we build brands from zero. We don't just do jingles, we create the whole system.'

and hospitality, alongside working as directors at Wieden+Kennedy. 'Our core skill now is partnership. We make good partners. We identify people whose sensibilities we share, who are really creative at what they do. We go to them, and just say that if you and we cross sensibilities, something great is going to happen. Now, let's work from there,' explains Jayal, adding, with a trademark lack of modesty, 'What we can do is we build brands from zero. We don't just do jingles, we create the whole system.'

For any creative-minded person, it is an ideal position to be in: to work alongside a trusted partner to build brands, within the boundaries of an agency structure, as well as having the freedom to explore entrepreneurial ventures outside the agency.

2 June 2015

UPDATE: *This is an updated version of a story that first appeared on 9 August 2012.*

Portraits of Wieden+Kennedy employees

PORTFOLIO LIVES

The notion of portfolio living–or managing a portfolio of activities, rather than one full-time job–is attributed to management thinker and author Charles Handy, who coined the term over two decades ago. In his 1989 book, *The Age of Unreason*, Handy is said to have predicted that knowledge workers would increasingly adopt 'a portfolio of activities–some we do for money, some for interest, some for pleasure, some for a cause . . . the different bits fit together to form a balanced whole greater than the parts.' Since then, there has been a rise in knowledge workers who have exchanged full-time employment for greater independence, and have the freedom to pursue a range of activities, for monetary and non-monetary reasons.

Although this is not normally a work style associated with senior executives, it was apparent that some industries lend themselves to 'portfolio living'. For example, art specialist Tasneem Zakaria Mehta holds several positions–as the honorary director of the Bhau Daji Lad museum, the vice chairman of art conservation non-profit Intach, as well as serving on the boards of several other art-related institutions and contributing regularly to newspapers.

Rajagopalan Balakrishnan and Prasoon Joshi capture different expressions of portfolio lives–alongside their primary roles as heads of their respective advertising agencies, both have established careers as film directors or writers. They must thus juggle managerial responsibilities alongside creative commitments to their clients and their producers.

Both workspaces operate as ateliers, or studios, for ideas, although they look different. Balakrishnan's office is compact and spare, with little apart from a discussion table, a television and a great view. Joshi's workspace is more spacious, and lined with trophies. Both deliver the same message: it's the idea that counts, nothing else.

PRASOON JOSHI

Prasoon Joshi says the awards displayed in his office relate to his advertising successes, those at home are for his literary achievements

THE CONNECTED CRAFTSMAN

Some offices hold few surprises, more insight. Such as the spacious executive office in an advertising agency in mid-town Mumbai. It has a dark carpet, clean, white surfaces, and a floor-to-ceiling wall of trophies, next to a meeting table. The formidable line-up of awards is predictable: The room's inhabitant, Prasoon Joshi, is a much applauded poet, songwriter, screenwriter, copywriter, executive chairman of McCann World group India and president of its South Asia regional arm.

Like many in his industry, Joshi is nomadic about his work location, and often works outside the office–at home, in hotel suites with his team, or by himself, using noise-cancelling headsets on planes. The office is clearly, however, his personalized workspace, a gallery of his achievements as well as a suite conducive for both group meetings and solitary work.

The 'rejection' gavel

Connecting brands and consumers

A range of objects on the cabinet behind

Joshi's desk captures his repertoire of work in both advertising and entertainment. There are mementoes from the brands and the films he has worked on, including General Motors and Chevrolet miniature cars, a tribute to the recently released film, *Bhaag Milkha Bhaag* (for which Joshi wrote the script and the lyrics), and a framed series of coins from ING commemorating a memorable advertising campaign. How does Joshi manage to weave the different strands of his professional work life together? He offers a straightforward answer: By constantly honing his ability to connect with people.

'The intelligent clients who come to me, they know the role of advertising and communication is connection. It's not that they do not know how to do business.'

'The intelligent clients who come to me, they know the role of advertising and communication is connection. It's not that they do not know how to do business. They're not coming to me for the same reason they're going to McKinsey. They're coming to me because I understand the business and I understand the consumer and I can be the bridge. And they see the examples of it, not only in advertising, through my work outside advertising also,' Joshi elaborates.

It is important to remember that while consumers might express feelings through brands, advertisements themselves are inherently intrusive, he states. 'You'd better have entertained me or informed me or added value to my life, otherwise you have no business to intrude,' he adds, jokingly raising a gavel, placed behind his desk, which he says he uses to reject mediocre work.

Mementoes from the film 'Bhaag Milkha Bhaag'

Joshi employs a number of tactics to 'sharpen his craft'. First, to keep in touch with popular culture, he makes it a point to interact with as many people as possible, whether addressing a crowd of thousands at the Jaipur Literature Festival, mingling with friends, family and locals in smaller towns, speaking with college youth during

Joshi's workspace is conducive for both group meetings and solitary work

events or just watching movies in cinemas to see audience reactions.

Second, he strongly endorses creative cross-pollination, where working on films can result in ideas for advertisements and vice versa. 'We're in the profession of communication, where we are dealing with words, images, poetry, music, popular culture. So anything I do in popular culture, it's only going to help.'

'Ads better have entertained me or informed me or added value to my life, otherwise they have no business to intrude.'

Finally, Joshi seeks to 'create filters' for himself by which he can understand his client's problems, and generate solutions. 'I believe in absorption. I don't take notes. I absorb. And I believe a system knows how to absorb and how much to keep and how to create filters. And those filters are very important for me. I soak myself into a brief but after a point, I don't need that.'

The idea generation process itself usually takes place in two stages–'gregarious' brainstorming in workshops with his colleagues and clients, followed by a more 'meditative' stage, where Joshi 'goes back and forth, chiselling and crafting the idea'.

Creative rewards

The line-up of trophies prompts a discussion about the value and significance of awards, often a controversial subject in the advertising industry. Those displayed in his office relate to his advertising successes, there are others at home from his literary career, he says.

'We're in the profession of communication, where we are dealing with words, images, poetry, music, popular culture. So anything I do in popular culture, it's only going to help.'

Joshi is clear about the merits as well as the hazards of industry awards. 'There are countless people who have started award shows. But there are very few which are of significance,' he states, pointing to a row of metal pencils and lion-shaped trophies from the One Show and the Cannes Lions Festival, respectively, both global advertising competitions.

'Pencils and Lions were very rare. . . now we keep winning these, so we feel very good about it,' Joshi says. He also highlights another, more old-fashioned-looking trophy. 'This is one of the first individual awards I won when I came to Bombay, it was given by the Radio and Production Association, which was a big organization then, many great voices came from it.'

Awards should serve simply as a motivator to enhance one's craftsmanship, professes Joshi. 'It's a platform where your tools can be sharpened, where you can be exposed to more and more ideas, which will help your everyday work.' Unhealthy competition or excessive one-upmanship are signs that the awards process is malfunctioning, he says.

The workshop

Joshi's references to craftsmanship remind me of a seminal book on the subject, *The Craftsman* (2008), by Richard Sennett, who describes craftsmanship as 'the desire to do a job well for its own sake' and involves 'accumulated learning,

Miniature cars and other mementoes dot the space behind his desk

'Awards are platforms where your tools can be sharpened, where you can be exposed to more and more ideas, which will help your everyday work.'

reflection, repetition and habit'–all traits exemplified by Joshi.

Joshi's workplace also seems to embody that of a master craftsman, according to Sennett, who says, 'In craftsmanship, there must be a superior who sets standards and who trains. For the craftsman, authority resides in the quality of his skills.' Joshi similarly states, 'Everybody who works with me, in a sense, respects what I've done. And looks up and comes to learn something from me.'

While Sennett goes on to advocate the virtues of craftsmanship as a template for life in general, he does include a cautionary note. Medieval workshops often did not endure because 'the master's originality inhibited knowledge transfer'. Luckily for Joshi, modern communication makes this much less of a challenge.

29 September 2013

Balakrishnan's clutter-free room with a view

RAJAGOPALAN BALAKRISHNAN

THE PAPERLESS, 'PORTFOLIO CAREER'

The office is compact–150 sq. ft–and ruthlessly spare, populated only by a centrally placed, glass-topped oval table, a pack of ordinary black task chairs and an unobtrusive flat-screen TV. A stand-alone desk and pedestal are consigned to a corner, serving as de facto baggage stands. Like airport lounges the world over, it appears transitional in nature, composed only of the bare essentials of seat and table–curiously unlike a space one would associate with the chairman of Lowe Lintas, one of India's largest advertising agencies.

Rajagopalan Balakrishnan, known universally as Balki, has occupied the corner office since 2003, when the entire workspace, situated on the fifteenth floor of Express Towers at Nariman Point, was last refurbished. He was national creative director at the time. After his elevation to the top spot in 2008, he decided against moving into his predecessor's generous suite, which now accommodates twenty-five people in an open-plan layout.

'I'll never move, I'll feel lonely in more space,' says Balakrishnan, professing that a quiet, clean office with 'a bare minimum sense of aesthetics' is all that he needs to get on with his job. 'An office needn't be

'I'll never move, I'll feel lonely in more space. A quiet, clean office with a bare minimum sense of aesthetics is all I need.'

zany because that's not the nature of advertising people, it's not the nature of advertising,' he says, a statement that grossly understates the millions of dollars that go into creating larger-than-life workplaces for creative agencies, whether in Mumbai, San Francisco or elsewhere. In fact, at the Lowe London office, visitors are greeted by a bar and cafe, placed right next to the front desk, instead of conventional meeting rooms.

Creative sans chaos

Balakrishnan's office appears to be underpinned by a radical notion: his apparent belief that creativity and efficiency can co-exist. He jettisons the outer frills to which advertising professionals often feel entitled. 'I like nothing to see, nothing to look at when I'm working, I even put the blinds down,' he says, adding, 'I don't even need a sheet of paper. Most of the time now, you say the idea'. His colleagues corroborate his approach to work. One co-worker describes him as 'a force of energy', almost chameleon-like in his ability to adapt to a given environment.

The stark emphasis on functionality also correlates with Balakrishnan's increasingly 'portfolio life' as full-time chairman and active film-maker. The term 'portfolio life' can be attributed to Charles Handy, a leading management thinker. In *Rethinking the Future,* a collection of prescient essays by management heavyweights such as Michael Porter and C.K. Prahalad, Handy predicted, in 1998, 'life will be a collection of different activities, like a share portfolio'.

Handy believed individuals would come to balance their working hours between activities that would nourish stomach and soul, i.e., earn a living and provide personal fulfillment. He envisaged a scenario where half the developed world's workforce 'will be working "outside" the organ-

Instead of a dedicated computer, he uses a computer in his assistant's office as and when required

ization' as temporary, part-time and contract workers.

Balakrishnan is one of the most visible examples of a thriving Indian portfolio life. Lowe Lintas continues to rank in the top five creative agencies in India. Over the last three years, he has written and directed two commercially successful feature films, *Cheeni Kum* and *Paa*. A film production house with his spouse, Gauri, is in the offing. This dual existence requires discipline and focus on first-time-right ideas. Balakrishnan says he manages by 'carefully sifting through the faff'–streamlining his day to concentrate on productive projects rather than having to rework ideas, entertain clients or attend motivation therapy workshops.

'I like nothing to see, nothing to look at when I'm working, I even put the blinds down. I don't even need a sheet of paper. Most of the time now, you say the idea.'

Physical demarcation of spaces helps. Films are written on weekends and evenings, from home, in a room with a treadmill and a cat, and usually edited at night. When directing, he takes time off from the advertising business to travel to shoots. In a 'regular advertising month', he says he spends half his working hours in the office–'We can sell scripts over the phone, which is fabulous'–rather than squandering time in traffic between meetings. He transcends modern

This dual existence requires discipline and focus on first-time-right ideas. Balakrishnan says he manages by 'carefully sifting through the faff'– to concentrate on productive projects.

computing, eschewing a laptop, parking himself at his assistant's computer when necessary.

Wielding his mobile, gliding from studio to film set to home office and office, Balakrishnan is not tethered to any one physical space–this too explains his underdressed cabin.

One rule for all

The deeper question is whether this system is replicable for others at Lowe Lintas. Lynda Gratton, professor of management practice at the London Business School, contends that such roles work well for organizations too, explaining that most portfolio careerists 'have interesting networks and introduce new ideas into companies'.

Balakrishnan says he encourages Lowe Lintas employees to seriously pursue other interests outside work, as long as 'they can balance both lives'. Several employees are aspiring painters, installation artists and screenplay writers.

In some ways, though, Lowe Lintas is traditional. It remains anchored in Express Towers, one of India's first skyscrapers and a bastion of the Indian corporate establishment, while many others have emigrated northwards. Yet, if it continues to grant its foot soldiers more flexibility, it will set itself apart as an employer of choice–and perhaps save a bit on office spending too.

2 May 2010

Mehta's museum office has a scholarly air

TASNEEM ZAKARIA MEHTA

THE RETAILER OF CULTURE

The most defining feature of Tasneem Zakaria Mehta's office at the Bhau Daji Lad Museum in Mumbai is unusual. It's not the antique furniture or the view of the sixth-century elephant statue, or even the double-height ceilings. It is 'celadon green', the subtle colour of the room's paint finish–the same colour which wraps the museum. The choice of shade tells a story of legacy and transformation, of past lives being made relevant to present circumstances.

Mehta is the managing trustee and honorary director of the city's oldest museum, established in 1855 and known as Mumbai's Victoria and Albert Museum until 1975. Unlike the other spaces and people featured in *Head Office*, the Bhau Daji Lad Museum is not a corporate entity, and Mehta is not a company chief executive. It is far more intriguing: a public institution funded by the municipal corporation of Greater Mumbai, actively supported by a leading private sector business family, the Bajaj family, and restored by a non-profit, the Indian National Trust for Art and Cultural Heritage

Mehta's offices have curated artefacts, such as the telephone

'It is such a profound historical space, has such a strong visual character to it, to put any contemporary interjection would be just too disruptive.'

(Intach). In Mehta's world, the public, private and non-profit appear to merge seamlessly.

Mehta is also Intach's vice chairman, a member of the governing council of Hyderabad's Salar Jung Museum, the chair of the Confederation of Indian Industries' task force on museums and heritage, and a regular contributor to newspapers. It's a packed 'portfolio life'.

Shades of green

Mehta's museum office was designed to echo its era. 'It is such a profound historical space, has such a strong visual character to it, to put any contemporary interjection would be just too disruptive,' she reasons. The cupboards and writing desk have been preserved; the new sofas, tables and pendant lights are aesthetically congruent. Modern technology (surveillance TV and computer equipment) do not detract from the scholarly air; I felt like I was walking into the office of a colonial school's headmistress.

Mehta says celadon green was considered 'the most appropriate colour for the contemplation of the arts' by Henry Cole, the first director of the V&A Museum in London and the architect of the Great Exhibition of 1851, the first international exhibition of culture and industry, which inspired the creation of the Mumbai museum. This 150-year-old fact was revealed during extensive research on the Victorian colour palette, an example of Mehta's aesthetic due diligence.

The walls of the museum are in celadon green, considered most appropriate for the contemplation of the arts by Henry Cole, the first director of the V&A Museum in London

Yet the colour green has another interpretation: as a metaphor for the museum's new, customer-oriented, revenue-maximizing strategy, led by Mehta. Since the museum reopened in January 2008, it has strengthened its dialogue with Mumbaikars–from primary school students to contemporary art collectors. Its current show is an

The lobby of the museum

example: an exhibition of life-size installations by artist Sudarshan Shetty–theatrical, ambitious and a crowd-puller.

Mehta says her curatorial instincts were honed during four formative years as a buyer with Bloomingdale's, New York City's famous department store. Retail is an unlikely path to museum management, even for someone with degrees in the fine arts, art history, liberal arts and English literature, but Mehta points out unexpected similarities between the two domains. 'You are engaged with the customer, you have to make that point of contact in both places. Here we're selling a ticket, we also have a shop, we have a cafe, exactly like Bloomingdale's,' she explains.

Museums today must entertain, as much as educate, in order to attract audiences, she says, emphasizing that 'in the beginning that was what museums were about'.

She agrees with me that museums today must entertain, as much as educate, in order to attract audiences, emphasizing that 'in the beginning that was what museums were about'.

Personal wares

Mehta's dual lives–as former retailer and current curator–are captured in her sea-facing home office in her eleventh-floor flat in a landmark Nariman Point residential building. The room is a collector's haven, bulging with racks of books, a

Mehta's home office is a collector's haven, with an eclectic selection of books, artwork, contemporary and antique furniture

disparate collection of paintings and photographs, and an eclectic selection of decorative objects and furniture of varying provenance. Antique chairs from London are juxtaposed with an experimental art furniture chair from Mumbai. A black and white portrait of her daughter by famed photographer Dayanita Singh hangs alongside works from lesser-known artists. Books on history, fiction, art and design jostle for space.

'I don't think you ever get to head an institution without understanding that you have different stakeholders, they have different concerns, which must be addressed.'

Yet every object has been carefully assigned its place, preserved with a curator's devotion, and monitored with a retailer's eagle eye ('Maintenance and management of objects is a huge issue, whether at home or in the museum,' she sighs).

The two offices demarcate Mehta's multiple roles. She spends mornings and late nights at home, responding to emails and phone calls, and writing. After a mandatory break for exercise late morning, she is at the museum until early evening.

When I wonder how she weaves together the different strands, her answer is deceptively straightforward. 'I don't think you ever get to head an institution without understanding that you have different stakeholders, they have different concerns, which must be addressed,' she states, explaining her ability to weld public, private and non-profit interests. Adding, 'When you are CEO in two or three capacities, then everything you do is directed towards work. There are no boundaries, one flows into the other.' Just like the design of the museum, with its harmonious blend of materials, objects, structure, space and time.

'When you are CEO in two or three capacities, then everything you do is directed towards work. There are no boundaries, one flows into the other.'

17 October 2010

UPDATE: *Mehta is no longer a member of the governing council of Hyderabad's Salar Jung Museum or the chair of the Confederation of Indian Industries' task force on museums and heritage.*

She is a member of the academic council of the National Museum Institute, on the governing board of the National Institute of Design, on the advisory board of the National Gallery of Modern Art and a member of the international council of New York's Museum of Modern Art.

RESILIENCE

Resilience, as a business term, is generally understood as an organizational competence or an ability to cope with external shocks and manage risks.

My interviews lead me to believe that the term can apply to chief executives too. One of the most interesting discoveries during my research was the way in which chief executives whose businesses had a strong regulatory interface came across as highly resilient. They were measured, patient, unruffled, understated and prepared for adversity, in general. They seem to recognize that it takes time to build assets, that there are factors beyond their control at all times, and that personal equilibrium must be maintained. This is clearly what it takes to succeed in these sectors.

Personal workplaces provided interesting clues about individual resilience. For G.V. Sanjay Reddy, managing director of infrastructure conglomerate GVK, his soundproof Mumbai office overlooking the airfield serves as a metaphor for his ability to stay calm amidst external activity and turbulence.

Similarly, the imperfectly constructed slanted walls in Vikram Limaye's office underline the problem of building world-class infrastructure in India. The workplace illustrates why the head of the Infrastructure Development Finance Corporation wants to work towards improved institutional architecture.

For Chitra Ramkrishna, the managing director of the National Stock Exchange, the decision not to open her personal space to media reveals much about her need to maintain boundaries, an important aspect of adopting a measured approach to growth.

Finally, Tata Steel managing director T.V. Narendran's pragmatism is captured in his office, which honours the past, while simultaneously looking to the future.

Ramkrishna prefers to meet visitors in a lounge-style meeting room

CHITRA RAMKRISHNA

THE MEASURED MARKET MAKER

This is one of the rare occasions for *Head Office* when I learn more about a person from what I don't see than from what I do see. The person in question is Chitra Ramkrishna, the chief executive officer of the Mumbai-based National Stock Exchange of India Ltd (NSE).

She preferred to meet me in her designated meeting room in the corporate executive suite rather than in her cabin. It is a trademark measured move on Ramkrishna's part–just enough to have a fruitful dialogue, yet not too intrusive for someone known to guard her privacy.

Several artefacts dot the room such as this Ganpati

Classic elegance

The meeting room resembles a gracious living room, with an eight-seater dining table, a set of sofas and armchairs, and a cabinet stacked with books and artefacts. It is a work setting that is found in several corporate executive suites, well suited for individual or small

'Dr Patil came from an institutional mindset. For him, if you were an established institution, you would need a building of your own, and this is what we could afford at the time.'

group meetings, especially with external visitors whom CEOs would prefer not to meet in their private workspace, and more conducive to conversation than a conference room.

Ramkrishna first used the room jointly with her predecessor Ravi Narain, now she tends to use it herself.

The objects in the cabinet are indicative of a rarefied set of interests: nineteenth-century English literary classics; books on wildlife; religious artefacts, including an intriguing Ganpati whose trunk seems to be balanced in thin air; team photographs; and official citations. The facing walls have historical photographs of Mumbai. 'A little bit of art and literature is always preferred,' says Ramkrishna, adding that Narain 'was fond of the photographs too.'

Outside, gleaming high-rise office towers make up the Bandra-Kurla Complex's iconic skyline. 'This was marshland when we first moved in here fourteen years ago,' says Ramkrishna, attributing the NSE's decision to invest in its own building to R.H. Patil, the exchange's first chief executive. 'Dr Patil came from an institutional mindset. For him, if you were an established institution, you would need a building of your own, and this is what we could afford at the time,' she explains.

Pioneering a new platform

The company's Exchange Plaza headquarters is a physical reflection of its status as a groundbreaking exchange. From its inception in the early 1990s, when Ramkrishna joined the company as part of the founding team, the NSE pioneered screen-based trading in India, enabling a new generation of stock market professionals to take part in securities trading. Today, over 80 per cent of all trading in derivatives and cash takes place on its platforms, and the company has been valued at over $3 billion (around ₹ 18,000 crores).

At a time when stock markets are so volatile, I am keen to ask Ramkrishna what it takes to successfully run an exchange.

The answer, it turns out, has three parts to it.

First, adopting a measured approach to growth. As an exchange, the NSE is necessarily market-led and responsive to customers. Equally, it is responsible to the regulatory authorities. So while deciding to pursue any new initiative, 'we have to look at all the constituencies, from the small broker to the large broker, from the issuer to potential investors, and to the regulator', Ramkrishna explains. 'We can't stop ourselves from doing things because it brings risks. The best thing to do is to mitigate those risks. It's our job to continuously move the envelope on greater risk mitigation, and our regulatory framework is more mindful of risks and compliance than many other markets.'

'Our biggest strength is we have a steady team, and all of them understand the nuances of the three pillars (business, technology and regulation) very well.'

A measured approach can only be achieved by clearly defining certain boundaries (such as her decision to protect the privacy of her cabin). She is similarly categorical and clear-cut about whether the NSE might like to issue an initial public offering: 'The board has always said at the right time we can look at it.' She declines to elaborate further.

Second, managing an exchange requires three different kinds of domain expertise–an understanding of business, regulation and technology. The latter is especially relevant as increasingly markets are being affected by new approaches to trading, such as 'high-frequency trading' or 'algorithmic trading' driven by computers, rather

Classics by authors like Thomas Hardy and Jane Austen are indicative of a wide range of interests

The National Stock Exchange headquarters in Mumbai

than human beings, which some perceive as potentially detrimental to the market.

'The one thing that has happened in the last two decades is that the exchange business is inevitably and irretrievably intertwined with technology,' says Ramkrishna. She points out that an understanding of products and technology needs to be woven together to serve customers. It cannot be one at the expense of the other.

'It's our job to continuously move the envelope on greater risk mitigation, and our regulatory framework is more mindful of risks and compliance than many other markets.'

Teamwork between the three functions–at both the senior leadership team and operating team levels–is critical, she says. 'Our biggest strength is we have a steady team, and all of them understand the nuances of the three pillars (business, technology and regulation) very well,' Ramkrishna says.

Apart from built-in interdependencies in job functions, the performance management mechanism rewards teams for collaboration, says Ramkrishna. Teamwork has certainly featured in this conversation more than it has with most chief executives for this column.

Catalysts for growth

Finally, managing an exchange is about playing a catalysing role in the ecosystem, providing the platform for the market to grow. 'This business is dependent on everyone else. Sure, we're running it, but the value has to be perceived by everyone–institutions, retail, brokers, companies, all of them,' Ramkrishna says. Financial inclusion remains an important goal; Ramkrishna acknowledges that the participation of retail investors in the market is low.

'This business is dependent on everyone else. Sure, we're running it, but the value has to be perceived by everyone–institutions, retail, brokers, companies, all of them.'

The NSE is a particularly interesting institution, since it must be market-responsive, customer-led and technology-driven, yet it is essentially a state-sponsored creation.

In my experience, there is a certain breed of professionals, like Ramkrishna, that is attracted to this sort of institutional role: those who are understated and restrained, able to shape public policy, committed to the public realm, and with a market-facing mindset. They are artful balancers, like the seemingly precarious Ganpati in her meeting room, a metaphor for staying still and upright. Such professionals usually also have a long-term view and a respect for history, captured by the historical photographs and novels in Ramkrishna's meeting room.

Her workplace in the landmark NSE building offers two lessons for anyone concerned with growing the Indian economy. First, it highlights how platforms like the NSE enable the growth of the ecosystem. Without a catalytic enabler like the NSE, the markets might not have grown. Second, it signifies how such platforms are themselves sources of tremendous value creation to their stakeholders, whether public or private.

A gift from a trip to Thailand

1 June 2014

G.V. SANJAY REDDY

Reddy's wood-panelled room looks out onto the airfield

THE COMPOSED MULTITASKER

Of all the workplaces I've visited in my series, this one serves as the most appropriate visual metaphor for its occupant and his work style. I'm seated in a peaceful, wood-panelled cabin–situated at the edge of an airfield in Mumbai, but well insulated from the roar and throttle of the aircraft outside.

His taste in art is 'traditional' and he has little interest in contemporary or modern Indian art

Its inhabitant, G.V. Sanjay Reddy, the vice chairman of GVK Power and Infrastructure Ltd, and managing director of Mumbai International Airport Pvt. Ltd, is equally calm and composed, with little to suggest that he is grappling with a storm of business challenges. Reddy is the son of G.V. Krishna Reddy, the founder chairman and managing director of the Hyderabad-based infrastructure conglomerate, the GVK group.

The power of positive thinking

Reddy's office is part of a senior management suite located in the domestic Terminal 1 at

Chhatrapati Shivaji International Airport, and accessed through an unobtrusive entrance between the departure and arrival gates. 'Being near the airfield and the terminal gates gives you a feel of the business and I think that was important, as opposed to just being in a beautiful building outside,' says Reddy. He first moved into the airport in 2006, when the GVK-led consortium was awarded the contract to modernize and develop the Mumbai airport. He and his colleagues initially worked out of a temporary workspace and moved into the current premises a couple of years later.

'Being near the airfield and the terminal gates gives you a feel of the business and I think that was important, as opposed to just being in a beautiful building outside'.

The classic C-suite combination of a wood-lined interior, brown leather sofas and a Kashmiri rug reflects Reddy's aesthetic preferences. 'We've developed a certain look and feel in all our offices. We like wood. We like it to be not so minimalistic,' he says.

Reddy's taste in art is similarly traditional. 'I don't have much interest in contemporary or modern Indian artists,' he says, adding that his Hyderabad office has several Tanjore paintings. The long-awaited T2 terminal of the Mumbai airport will have a 1.2 km 'art wall' of traditional and modern Indian art, an aspect of the airport modernization project that is particularly important to the detail-oriented Reddy. He hopes that it will capture 'the expanse, depth and beauty of Indian art'.

A dagger gifted by an Indonesian associate

Potted plants carefully placed on tiny mats convey serenity; Reddy says he 'loves landscaping and greenery, something small that will keep the room lively'. Reddy's demeanour is equally sanguine. The day before our meeting (in May), Reddy's flagship company, GVK Power and Infrastructure Ltd, declared significant losses for the financial year ended March. The GVK group

The plans for Chhatrapati Shivaji International Airport, Mumbai are framed and displayed behind Reddy's desk

also has huge debt (in excess of ₹ 15,000 crores), the share price of the flagship company is currently trading poorly and its ambitious Australian coalmining project in Queensland is battling falling coal prices. Isn't he a little bit stressed?

'If I think I'm doing great, I feel great also. I consciously decided a few years ago that I will have to work on disassociating my mind from the state of the business. I have to.'

The answer is a firm no, for two reasons. First, at a personal level, Reddy says he has learnt to leverage 'the power of positive thinking. If I think I'm doing great, I feel great also. I consciously decided a few years ago that I will have to work on disassociating my mind from the state of the business. I have to. My state of mind cannot be determined by the state of the business,' he emphasizes.

Second, stress is an occupational hazard. The nature of the infrastructure business entails that many critical success factors are beyond the control of managers, such as the availability of gas supply to their power plants, Reddy explains, adding that the priority is to remain focused on execution. Alongside commissioning a new terminal at Mumbai airport, Reddy is aiming to complete the expansion of the Bangalore airport terminal, and to commission two power projects and a toll road project before the end of the financial year. 'This year is critical for us. Once these projects all go into operation and start generating cash flow, then I think we won't have much of an issue to worry about,' he predicts.

'Our DNA is that we are used to getting into new businesses, understanding those businesses, creating excellence in those businesses. And it happens every few years. It's not new. I think we are true entrepreneurs.'

Airport loungelife

The office, with its view of planes in perpetual motion, is a visual metaphor in other ways too. Its clean look and minimal personal items make it resemble a business traveller's airport lounge–not unlike those that Reddy might frequent on an almost daily basis. Reddy says he is 'literally on the move. I average one flight a day and sometimes don't visit my base office in Hyderabad in two or three weeks.' He says he has learnt to work on the move, through electronic gadgets and conference or video calls, as well as meetings in the car while on the road. He divides his time primarily between Australia, Hyderabad, Mumbai and Delhi.

Just like the aeroplanes that land and take off from their destinations, Reddy himself dives in and out of business operations, depending on each company's requirements at a particular point in time. He's based more in Mumbai at the moment, as the project is at a critical phase of execution leading up to the terminal's opening later this year.

This nomadic existence is a direct consequence of the group's geographical and sideways expansion into new, often unrelated industries, with escalating scale, the logic of which some commentators have questioned. Over the last fifteen years, the GVK group has expanded from running hotels, to setting up power plants, modernizing airports, building roads and finally, investing in a coal mine in Australia last year.

The University of Michigan-educated Reddy

'The effort is to try to see how to kick myself out of this job. I always tell my people, I consider myself most successful when things get done when I'm not even once involved.'

acknowledges that specialization and focus, rather than diversification, are essential tenets of any MBA programme. But, he caveats, 'Our DNA is different. Our DNA is that we are used to getting into new businesses, understanding those businesses, creating excellence in those businesses. And it happens every few years. It's not new. I think we are true entrepreneurs.'

Reddy prides his conglomerate's execution skills and the ability to refresh industry standards. 'I had no clue about coal mining two years ago. Today I can tell you, the chart that we set out in coalmining is completely different from what traditional companies are doing,' he says.

His approach is to throw himself into new projects, build a team to manage the project and then enable them to execute. 'The effort is to try to see how to kick myself out of this job. I always tell my people, I consider myself most successful when things get done when I'm not even a little involved,' he summarizes. An apt philosophy for a global multitasker, and one that will be put to the test when Mumbai's new terminal opens.

25 August 2013

UPDATE: *Terminal 2 was inaugurated in January 2014, and operations began in February 2014.*

A potted plant in Reddy's cabin

Narendran's presidential desk with seven visitor chairs

T.V. NARENDRAN

THE RESILIENT PRAGMATIST

There are some C-suites where the message appears to be deceptively simple: it just doesn't get more traditional than this. One such example is Tata Steel's India office in Jamshedpur, Jharkhand, where I am meeting T.V. Narendran, managing director (India and South East Asia).

Narendran is a company lifer–he joined the company in 1988 as a campus recruit from the Indian Institute of Management, Calcutta. After twenty-five years of working in the company, in different roles in different parts of the world, many of which included marketing and sales assignments, he was appointed managing director in November 2013.

A framed 'cover' of the *Economist* magazine

Tata Steel has a tripartite management leadership structure. Hence Narendran works alongside two other business heads–group executive director Koushik Chatterjee, who is responsible for finance and corporate functions and is based in the Mumbai headquarters, and Karl Ulrich Koehler, who heads Tata Steel Europe as its managing director and chief executive.

'Tata Steel has a certain culture and history, but what makes us competitive in the future is not necessarily what has kept us competitive in the past.'

Modernity amidst legacy

Legacy manifests itself through every possible design element in Narendran's private office on the first floor of one of the several low-rise factory buildings: the sprawling room has a presidential desk with seven visitor chairs, leather upholstered furniture, wood-panelled decor, classic artwork by artists such as Jehangir Sabavala, and multiple portraits of several generations of Tatas, including Jamsetji Tata and J.R.D. Tata.

There is every possibility that the cabin looked exactly the same when it was first created, about fifty years ago. Narendran is probably one of the few chief executives who can point out where at least four of his predecessors, including Hemant Nerurkar, B. Muthuraman, J.J. Irani and Russi Mody, occupied their offices (some in this room, others further down the corridor, he says).

In his office, two unusual objects catch my eye. First, a framed picture of what appears to be the cover of *The Economist* magazine, with the headline: 'T.V. Narendran. The world awaits your decision.' The headline seems to suggest Narendran had made it to the cover of the global magazine.

'I'd been a subscriber for a long time, and I didn't renew the subscription. So this is what they sent me; it's a marketing tool. I guess most people see the cover and write a cheque,' Narendran laughs. The decision to frame The Economist cover underlines Narendran's appreciation of a clever marketing and sales tactic.

A historic portrait

Second, a contemporary, stylized steel sculpture of a tree, resting on a shelf near the window, which captures steel's inherent strength as well as its flexibility. 'It was a gift from a distributor,' says Narendran, adding that he found it visually appealing.

Both items stand out as twin sparks of modernity in the overwhelmingly traditional room. They serve as a visual metaphor for Narendran's approach to his current job: introduce elements of change and modernity, without disrupting a century-old business legacy. This is particularly relevant given that the steel business in the country is increasingly vulnerable to external factors, whether lower prices, increased Chinese imports, or protracted land acquisition that can delay a new project by several years.

'We want to aim to have at least 25 per cent EBITDA margin with raw materials at market price. It's not that we know exactly how to reach there, but we said that unless we aim for that goal, and work towards it, we can't be competitive ten years or fifteen years from now.'

Change through resilience

Change, it appears, is predicated on making the business more resilient to fluctuating business circumstances. Narendran appears to be building resilience in three ways, all of which are centred on intangible assets such as nourishing his personal energy and building organizational capital.

The first element is a certain amount of pragmatism about change. 'Tata Steel has a certain culture and history, but what makes us competitive in the future is not necessarily what has kept us competitive in the past. It is like trying to turn a ship which is used to moving in a certain way,' says Narendran, adding that last year's ban on iron ore mining, which has now been lifted, accelerated the need for change. The company realized that without its captive iron ore mines, which served as raw materials for its steel manufacturing plants, it was far less profitable.

A steel tree sculpture

'We were at 30 per cent EBITDA (earnings before interest, taxes, depreciation and amortization) margin when our mines were running full on. We had 20 per cent EBITDA margin when most of the raw material was bought. And so we said that,

The wood-panelled room with extensive seating

over the next few years, we want to aim to have at least 25 per cent EBITDA margin with raw materials at market price. That's the goal we've set ourselves. It's not that we know exactly how to reach there, but we said that unless we aim for that goal, and work towards it, we can't be competitive ten years or fifteen years from now,' he says.

'There will be many things which will go wrong, not to be pessimistic or negative, but you brace yourself for some unpleasant surprises.'

Narendran is a pragmatist; he says he has learnt to assume 'that there will be many things which will go wrong, not to be pessimistic or negative, but you brace yourself for some unpleasant surprises'.

Inclusivity and agility

Second, a resilient business must necessarily be inclusive and collaborative, and rely on intangibles such as organizational capital, including people, processes structures and culture, so that it can react to change.

'This crisis on mining was not fantastic from a bottom-line perspective, but it was fantastic in the way the team worked together. We are not designed or set up to import raw material, but the organization saw that for the first time in 100 years all our mines were closed, but the steel plant did not close, because all the teams–raw materials, plant, procurement, legal, operations–worked seamlessly,' says Narendran.

'The crisis on mining was not fantastic from a bottom-line perspective, but it was fantastic in the way the team worked together.'

Finally, resilience needs agility to be effective. Narendran compares certain aspects of running a steel business to driving a car on the highway; with one car ahead and one car behind, one must remain agile and adjust one's speed so that one can always maintain distance, in order to avoid crashing.

For example, when running NatSteel, a Singapore-based steel company acquired by Tata Steel in 2005, Narendran learnt that 'the most important thing is to manage your exposure. Suppose I had three months' worth of orders booked at fixed price, I need to make sure that I have a three-month coverage of either inventory or raw materials. If I manage that well, then at least my input cost is guaranteed, and my realization is guaranteed. You need to manage that quite well and in a very hands-on way, similar to driving the car on a highway.' It is an approach that he continues to apply in his current role.

Tata Steel currently faces significant challenges –it posted a consolidated net loss of ₹ 3926 crores in 2014-15 against a net profit of ₹ 3595 crores in the previous year, domestic steel prices are under pressure and its balance sheet remains highly leveraged. But perhaps that is even more reason to remain resilient; and weld together a combination of pragmatism, collaboration and agility–a trio that might benefit any business, not just industrial-era ones.

22 June 2015

A decorated helmet given as a gift

VIKRAM LIMAYE

Limaye on the sixth-floor executive office, where partitions are positioned at an angle

THE PATIENT CATALYST

Something unusual catches my eye in a sixth-floor corporate office in Mumbai's Bandra Kurla Complex: the slanted walls that have been placed deliberately at an angle to the floor throughout the entire sixth-floor executive suite, perhaps to serve as a dynamic visual element.

This is the office of Vikram Limaye, CEO of Infrastructure Development Finance Corp. (IDFC) Ltd, one of the country's largest infrastructure lenders and a diversified financial services firm. Limaye first occupied the space in 2009 as executive director, when the corporate headquarters moved from Ramon House in south Mumbai, and continues to work out of it after becoming the head of the firm in 2013.

Leadership awards that Limaye has collected over the years

Although the design of the slanted walls is an innovative and well-meaning concept, its execution is flawed, with visible imperfections in detailing and construction. 'We're not happy with it either. The finishing is not up to the mark,' Limaye concurs with my observation. The office itself is serene, well lit and spacious, but pedestrian, like most bankers' workspaces. It has the usual mix of furniture and furnishings: a desk, a chair, a six-seater meeting table, a couple of armchairs, limited art, a few shelves of office-related artefacts and videoconferencing facilities.

'There have to be appropriate risk-sharing mechanisms between government and private sector, enough capacity within government to be able to regulate and monitor what risks are being shared, and how the country's resources are allocated.'

Architecture for growth

The imperfect interior architecture could serve as a metaphor for the business of infrastructure itself: Despite being a sector that attracts highly intelligent and ambitious people (including policymakers, entrepreneurs and financiers), execution has often been flawed and inadequate, especially in recent times, as it has struggled to fulfil the growing demands of an emerging economy.

Limaye responds with candour to this bleak assessment. 'Things have pretty much been at a standstill for the last twelve to eighteen months, so they can't get worse,' he says. 'We're learning from our mistakes. There have to be appropriate risk-sharing mechanisms between government and private sector, enough capacity within government to be able to regulate and monitor what risks are being shared, and how the country's resources are allocated,' he says. Lower risk will allow a broader pool of infrastructure entrepreneurs to enter the sector, help financiers to diversify lending risks and increase asset creation, he explains.

The right building blocks

It is an optimistic, big-picture argument, based on institutional reform. 'If we want the private sector to play such a large role in our country's development and in asset creation, we require the right

Limaye's sunlit cabin is utilitarian

institutional architecture,' Limaye reiterates at several points in our discussion.

Institutional reform in itself is not a new suggestion to drive economic growth, but Limaye's working style provides insight into how we might get there. First, he is patient and prepared to take the long-term view. For example, an industry insider tells me that Limaye prefers to wait and watch rather than participate in any very risky transaction.

'The infrastructure story is only a decade old.'

'The infrastructure story is only a decade old,' Limaye reminds me, emphasizing that the underlying factors that drive growth take time to mature. His substantial nine-year tenure at IDFC, since he first joined as an executive director in March 2005, appears to give him better perspective than most. Since 2005, Limaye has seen IDFC's balance sheet grow fourteen times, net worth nine times and profit after tax six times: a solid basis for a long-term view.

Second, he knows the importance of dexterity. IDFC was created with government support, specifically to catalyse private sector infrastructure growth. As its head, Limaye must necessarily juggle different viewpoints and stakeholders at all times. For example, IDFC must finance projects and deliver public goods while ensuring adequate returns for the private sector. Even within the firm, there are business units with differing objectives, such as the firm's commercial lending business, which lends to private sector entrepreneurs, and its public policy advisory unit that advises government on infrastructure policy.

'We're obviously very actively engaged with government to move policy along, to make sure we revisit some of the risk sharing, to see if we can expedite how infrastructure gets created.'

'We're obviously very actively engaged with government to move policy along, to make sure we revisit some of the risk sharing, to see if we can expedite how infrastructure gets created. It's a very rare situation where you're involved in a meaningful way with policy; when you're advising the government, it has ramifications on your business. We've been able to draw that line. We still are trusted and counted upon by the government to give objective policy advice,' he says about the firm's public policy unit.

This dexterity, of retaining the institution's credibility while continuing to grow and serve multiple stakeholders, is key to institutional reform for any organization in the infrastructure space.

Values create value

Finally, Limaye's understated personality defines his approach to building an institution. He points to a trophy on his shelf, an in-house IDFC award where employees nominated Limaye as a 'value champion' for 'nurturing humility'. His colleagues confirm that he is an approachable leader, not one prone to making lofty vision statements, but succinct, driven and continually focused on enhancing the firm's capabilities.

'I would want IDFC to be a high-performing, gold-standard, respected and trusted institution and a magnet to attract talent, with a culture that is intellectual, tolerant, informal and open,'

Limaye says. It is a long wish list, and if IDFC is issued a banking licence in the near future, the wish list will only get longer. Limaye patiently acknowledges the challenges. 'It's a journey, it can't happen overnight.'

Limited works of art like this M.F.Husain print dot Limaye's workspace

To some, Limaye's earnestness and diligence might seem mundane. But in a world where capital is notoriously impatient, and where institutional failure has been responsible for stifling India's economic growth, Limaye's prescription could serve as a robust foundation for the future.

9 February 2014

SPIRITUALITY

Spirituality is not commonly construed to be a business tool, as it is associated more often with philanthropy, or as a retirement vocation. Yet it is an element of daily business practice for several business leaders, including Kumar Mangalam Birla, the chairman of the Aditya Birla group of companies, and Ajay Piramal, the chairman of the Piramal group of companies, both of which are diversified industrial conglomerates.

Birla and Piramal draw on the *Bhagavad Gita* for business inspiration in several ways, which include developing greater mindfulness and equanimity during business negotiations, as well as cultivating a sense of legacy through the notion of long-term trusteeship.

These work styles are echoed in contemporary business management literature, which emphasizes emotional intelligence as an essential leadership trait. For example, renowned psychologist Daniel Goleman, writing in *What Makes A Leader?*, published in 2004 in the *Harvard Business Review*, explained that emotional intelligence comprised five specific skills: self-awareness, self-regulation, motivation, empathy and social skill. Many of these skills, including self-awareness, self-regulation and motivation in particular, are just as central to ancient Indian notions of spirituality as they are to business management literature.

These values are reflected in their physical work environment. The C-suites of both Birla and Piramal are archetypes for contemporary 'spiritual business retreats'–luxurious and refined in form, calm and peaceful in mood and atmosphere.

AJAY PIRAMAL

A curated art collection and selected religious artefacts lend a peaceful air to Piramal's workspace

THE SPIRITUAL NEGOTIATOR

For once, *Head Office* takes me to a familiar destination–a corporate office where I have attended workshops, listened to *bhajans* and even celebrated my wedding. This is the tenth floor of an office block in Lower Parel, Mumbai, and its inhabitant is my paternal uncle, Ajay Piramal, chairman of the Piramal Group, which is valued at over ₹ 18,000 crores. The group has interests in pharmaceuticals, real estate, financial services and data analytics.

A Buddha statue

Piramal shares the corporate floor with his wife Swati–they have different offices–and a handful of key executives. I am visiting with a specific objective in mind: to understand the link between workspaces, spirituality and negotiation. Piramal, having completed transactions with multinationals such as Abbott (2010) and Vodafone (2014), has adequate experience in the art of negotiating. I'm curious to know if his workspace provides any clues to his work style.

Space for serenity

The chairman's floor is marked by tranquillity and spaciousness. This is one of the few corporate offices I know of whose corridors themselves are large enough to stage a small music performance or host a family gathering. 'It is a luxury. Frankly, today in Mumbai you can't have such large corridors that are vacant,' Piramal says, adding that 'the large expanse leads to peace and quiet, which is important.' Piramal's private office is equally generous–a sunlit room with a large desk, armchairs and a coffee table, a marble floor and Kashmiri rugs.

'When you meditate, you have an erect body and are actually looking into your heart, looking down. An office should also be a place for contemplation.'

A curated and constantly evolving collection of modern artwork, including paintings by masters like F.N. Souza and Ram Kumar, and a sculpture of Mahatma Gandhi on the Dandi March, lines the corridors. For his office, Piramal selected a Jehangir Sabavala painting of birds flying (for its 'quiet and calm'), a classic Jamini Roy work of Rabindranath Tagore and Gandhi ('it is nationalistic') and a portrait of Hindu god Krishna (Piramal is an ardent believer and has been studying the *Bhagavad Gita* and other spiritual texts for over a decade). A brass statue of a seated Buddha, looking down, is placed at the entrance of his cabin. Piramal says he likes it for its posture: 'When you meditate, you have an erect body and are actually looking into your heart, looking down. An office should also be a place for contemplation.' He also has many images of Hindu gods and goddesses arranged on his desk.

The centrepiece of the office, and the prompt for the conversation, is a series of granite sculptures by artist Adwaita Gadanayak, placed at various intervals across the tenth floor, including in Piramal's personal workspace. Each sculpture depicts a particular verse from the *Bhagavad Gita*, selected by Piramal, and communicates a specific message

The chairman's floor is marked by tranquillity and spaciousness

that is relevant to business life.

For example, in Piramal's cabin, a stylized collection of sculpted stones is displayed museum-style, depicting that moment in chapter eleven in the *Bhagavad Gita* when Krishna displays his *vishwaroop* or universal form to the warrior prince Arjun. Piramal had it placed in clear line of sight, directly across the room from his desk to be able to 'see Krishna'.

'The Gita has been told to a warrior who is young, who is in the midst of a battle, full of emotions. In life, there are always intense battles, and yet we must practise the lessons from the Gita.'

Spirituality at work

Our walk around the office, and ensuing discussion, lead me to believe that there are at least three ways in which a spiritual practice is relevant to Piramal, the negotiator.

First, spirituality is as integral to his business philosophy as deal-making is to his business acumen. Piramal points to the conference room, which is named Partha (another name for Arjun). 'All our conference rooms are named after Arjun. We are disciples of Krishna and we look at ourselves like Arjun in the battlefield. Our philosophy always teaches us that you can have intense activity but inside you have to have peace. The office has to reflect that.'

Some might consider this to be a far-fetched statement, but Piramal re-emphasizes the application of the *Bhagavad Gita* to daily life. 'The *Gita* has not been told to a person who is living right up in the Himalayas. It has been told to a warrior who is young, who is in the midst of a battle, full of emotions. In life, there are always intense battles, and yet we must practise the lessons from the Gita.'

'If you concentrate on action and forget the results, you actually perform much better, because then you are not worried about what will happen.'

Second, spirituality fosters mindfulness and equanimity, which are vital in any negotiation as they help in being clear-headed. Piramal cites the famous *shlok* of the *Bhagavad Gita* (chapter two, verse forty-seven) that prescribes working for the means, not the fruit of one's action. 'If you concentrate on action and forget the results, you actually perform much better, because then you are not worried about what will happen. If you don't concentrate on action, either you start dreaming too much or get worried,' he says.

Focusing on the process is 'the most powerful thing to do in any negotiation', he says, adding that it leads to greater value creation. For example, one of the fundamental rules of any negotiation is that multiple options create greater value; an axiom that can only be implemented if one remains mindful during the negotiations. 'We do that all the time. How do we create win-win options? That's how I found that we always gain, to understand what is in the interest of the other party and which may not cost us so much,' Piramal explains.

Jaya Row, a well-known Vedanta scholar and *Bhagavad Gita* exponent, endorses this approach. A central message of the *Bhagavad Gita* is that clarity and equanimity, along with the strength of a powerful intellect, allows for better decision-making, especially in uncertain times, she says in a phone interview.

A sculpture of Gandhi on the Dandi March

Focusing on the process is 'the most powerful thing to do in any negotiation,' he says, adding that it leads to greater value creation.

Finally, Piramal uses the notion of trusteeship in the *Bhagavad Gita* to guide his sense of legacy. 'The beauty of the concept of trusteeship is that you don't look at your own benefit. You have to look at the benefit of all shareholders; there is no question of ego in it,' he says. This approach frees him from being too attached to any one asset or business.

Some have argued that this approach, of continuously buying and selling companies, can be confusing as it becomes difficult to understand the group's business direction. Piramal disagrees: 'We will do whatever is in the best interest of the shareholders. We keep evolving. None of our businesses were our old family business. If you don't change, if you don't evolve, you remain with the past.'

This approach doesn't preclude mistakes. Piramal acknowledges that there have been times 'when we negotiated too hard and the other side walked away' or 'when we bought a dud company and spent years fixing it', but a focus on process, over outcome, has helped him to learn from failures.

Many offices have a temple of worship, but this one is a tribute to our inner battlefields and our divinity. By integrating spiritual belief with business *buddhi* (business insight), Piramal is trying to align head, heart and hand in daily life.

31 May 2015

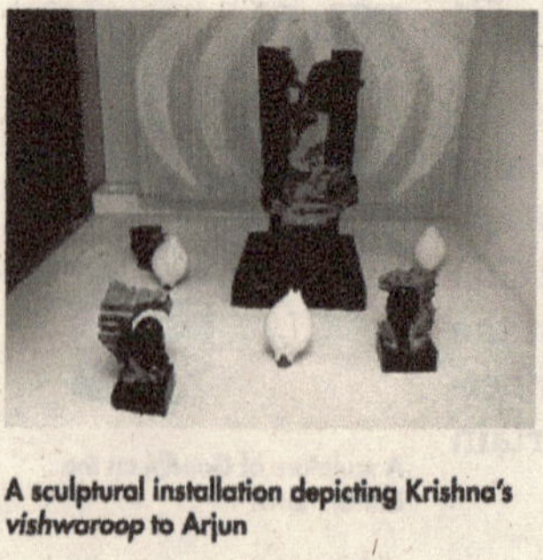

A sculptural installation depicting Krishna's *vishwaroop* to Arjun

Kumar Mangalam Birla says his workspace is relaxing but not laid-back

KUMAR MANGALAM BIRLA

THE BRAND CUSTODIAN

A long, arched corridor welcomes me to the chairman's floor at the corporate headquarters of one of India's largest conglomerates, in Mumbai's Worli district. These are the offices of the Aditya Birla Group of companies, which has interests in commodities, telecom, retail and financial services, among other industries.

Chairman Kumar Mangalam Birla and his team of executive assistants share the floor with Birla's mother, Rajashree Birla, who serves on the board of major group companies and heads the group's corporate social responsibility efforts.

At home

Although Birla prefers to conduct meetings in a conference room across the corridor, he takes us into his room. I hope to see a personalized workspace with interesting objects, and Birla's space doesn't disappoint.

A series of team photographs

It is extensive, with three distinct work

'I am very disciplined about doing important reviews for each business, especially all the large ones, say, about twelve to fourteen of them, I would review every quarter.'

settings–a desk, sofas and armchairs, and a round meeting table (which looks as though it could easily double up as a dining table). It is aesthetically and geographically diverse, with a mix of European furniture, lights and accessories, Chinese artefacts and Indian modern art, including a painting by M.F. Husain and idols of Hindu gods.

And it combines heritage and modernity. An old-fashioned leather trunk, stained-glass lighting fixtures and a globe are juxtaposed with contemporary furniture and furnishings. There are also several photographs of Birla's family, including those of his great-grandfather, his grandparents, his parents, wife Neerja and three children, as well as many photographs with colleagues.

The luxurious space reflects Birla's most visible attributes: his enduring ranking as one of India's wealthiest and most successful businesspeople, and his century-old Marwari business legacy.

Yet my lasting impression is not of the suite's grandeur but of its stillness, its calm and collected atmosphere. Perhaps it is the rows of green planters arranged on an adjoining terrace, or the afternoon light filtering in through the curtains, or Birla's no-rush approach, but the room seems unusually meditative.

Sometimes, the most dynamic people are fortified with a layer of Zen-like calm. Birla appears to be one of them. 'I hope that my spaces would relax those who come in here. I want them to look much more like an apartment, as opposed to officious-looking spaces,' he says. Birla adds, 'It's nice to be informal, eclectic, but at the same time it's a proper work environment. There's nothing casual about it, it's not a laid-back kind of space because that's not the kind of person I am.'

A collection of photographs and awards

Managing intangibles

The interplay of Birla's tangible workspace and its intangible work environment is promising. I am curious to understand whether this interplay can serve as a metaphor for his working style, and shed some light on the practical aspects of building intangible assets like organizational culture, which are becoming important value drivers for businesses.

'There are about 100 "high-potential" people on my radar. I would be intensely involved with which assignment they would go to next, what skill gaps they would require to fill in to take on that larger profit and loss, head of business kind of role.'

As we speak, it becomes clear that just like any other big business group, Birla operates through a series of 'tangible' frameworks and constructs–budgeting and planning cycles, quarterly reviews and strategic decision-making interventions–through which he monitors and manages a group with over 1,20,000 employees and $40 billion (around ₹ 2.5 trillion) in revenue, half of which emanates from operations outside India.

For example, Birla says: 'We have a very rigorous process of budgeting, a lot of quality time is spent on thinking the plan through. Then those numbers become sacrosanct.' Or 'I am very disciplined about doing important reviews for each business, especially all the large ones, say, about twelve to fourteen of them, I would review every quarter.' He decides his level of involvement with a particular business decision: depending on whether 'I need to know and therefore I'm involved, or I believe I need to be involved so that I can guide or add value'.

Yet what seems to animate these management constructs is a series of intangibles: emotional intelligence, spiritual belief and a sense of legacy, as reflected in the photographs, art and objects in his room, each of which hold clues to Birla's work style.

Several family photos and classic works of art are displayed in the C-suite

'My great-grandfather (G.D. Birla) always believed in the trusteeship concept of management, where you are managing as a trustee for shareholders.'

Emotional intelligence
Renowned psychologist Daniel Goleman says the 'most effective leaders are alike in one crucial way: They all have a high degree of what has come to be known as emotional intelligence.' Writing in *What Makes A Leader?*, published in 2004 in the *Harvard Business Review*, he explained that emotional intelligence comprised five specific skills: self-awareness, self-regulation, motivation, empathy and social skill.

Birla's approach to his people suggests that these skills are well honed. For example, when asked about the extent to which he really knows his people, given the size of the organization, he replies: 'There are about 100 "high-potential" people on my radar. I would be intensely involved with which assignment they would go to next, what skill gaps they would require to fill in to take on that larger profit and loss, head of business kind of role. So essentially what we are doing is not just working towards the success of the organization, but also helping people, setting them up for success.'

It is an important recognition that organizations can, and should, enable employees to perform, not simply expect employees to do so.

Spiritual belief
The nourishing atmosphere of the workplace can also perhaps be attributed to Birla's own equanimity. Having studied the *Bhagavad Gita* for many years, he says: 'I've come to believe that you do your best and then just leave the rest, as they say. You have to flow. And I think that's huge because it takes a huge burden off your shoulders. So I don't carry work home, I don't keep worrying about it, because my own philosophy is that I really work hard. And everyone here works very hard. And after that, if you

A family photograph

Birla's office space has three distinct work settings and a lot of greenery

worry, does that mean you think you can control everything? You can't.'

Birla is known to have a long-term approach to business, and is said to think of himself as a custodian of the brand and its values. 'My great-grandfather (G.D. Birla) always believed in the trusteeship concept of management, where you are managing as a trustee for shareholders. And I think your personal attributes, especially that of a promoter, do spill on to how the organization shapes up,' he says.

'I think that promoter-driven companies have an innate ability to take much higher risks, partly because of the fact that you have longer time horizons.'

This approach has strategic business benefits, he believes. 'I think that promoter-driven companies have an innate ability to take much higher risks, partly because of the fact that you have longer time horizons.'

Birla's 'tangible' stature and family legacy is almost impossible to emulate. His 'intangible' working style, however, has much to offer to any manager.

22 March 2015

SECTION II: ORGANIZATIONAL CAPITAL

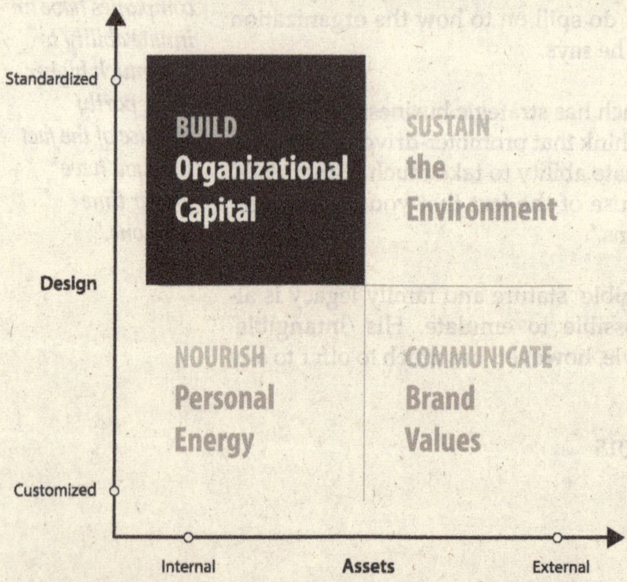

TOOLS TO BUILD ORGANIZATIONAL CAPITAL

C-suites have generally become smaller over time, so it was unsurprising to observe that several chief executives of large companies are comfortable working out of fairly compact offices. I was, however, intrigued to learn that some private offices had ceased to exist—a few chief executives now work out of open-plan workstations, just like the rest of their colleagues. Their work environments are informal, connected and democratic. Meetings take place in a variety of spaces, including in enclosed meeting rooms, at informal breakout areas or in the well-stocked company cafeteria.

For this band of business leaders, workplaces are more than items of capital expenditure; they are tools to drive organizational change. This applies as much to their personal workspaces as it does to the rest of the office. For example, for some chief executives **agility** or **collaboration** are key elements of workplace strategy. For others, a workplace is a modern-day studio for **craftsmanship** or a way to align their organization around their stated **purpose**. Finally, some business leaders employ the power of **integrative thinking** to align commerce with creativity at work.

Why invest in work culture

'Organizations offering the best places to work produce better returns on shareholder equity than their more ordinary counterparts,' writes James Heskett, a management professor at Harvard Business School, in his book, *The Culture Cycle: How to Shape the Unseen Force that Transforms Performance* (2011).

Effective workplaces promote healthy work cultures. Heskett's research leads him to conclude that 'as much as half of the difference in operating profit between organizations can be attributed to effective cultures, ...which can be a significant competitive advantage in bad times.'

A strong culture cannot be duplicated, professes Heskett. 'In many organizations, culture is the most potent and hard to replicate source of competitive advantage—far more important, for example, than technological innovation. By the time the superior performance it produces comes to the attention of the competitors and public, an organization's culture is well established and doing its job,' he says.

Researchers José Emilio Navas López et al. from the Universidad Complutense de Madrid agree. 'The elements that constitute the organizational capital of the firm, namely its culture, structure, organizational learning, and processes can be a source of competitive advantage,' they write in an eponymous research paper on organizational capital.

Valuable reasons as to why companies must design tangible workplaces, which shape intangible assets, and drive financial results.

DESIGN TRIGGERS FOR AN 'ENABLING' WORKPLACE:

1. *Would you like to be seated in the open-plan office, alongside other colleagues?*
2. *Would you be comfortable with a free seating arrangement, where others could use your workspace when you are travelling?*
3. *Would you like your office design to communicate that you are a flatter organization?*
4. *How would you like to leverage technologies to improve mobility at work?*
5. *Would you like to choose from multiple settings to conduct meetings, such as formal, enclosed meeting rooms, breakout spaces or semi-enclosed discussion spaces?*
6. *How will your workplace capture your organization's work culture?*
7. *How will your organization's values be captured in your workspaces?*

AGILITY

WORKSTYLE

Change management is an essential requirement in the job description of any chief executive, but offices are generally seen as static resources, physically difficult to move. So it was refreshing to meet a new breed of chief executives, for whom agility at work is an important driver of business success, and where the workplace itself enables flexibility and dynamism.

A growing number of senior professionals are almost nomadic at work; a trend that is a logical extension of mobile technology, open-plan offices and busy travel schedules. For example, Subroto Bagchi, chairman and co-founder of IT company Mindtree, works out of a conference room that is available to others to use in his absence.

Management professor, author and micro-entrepreneur Lynda Gratton leverages technology, especially collaborative digital tools and techniques, to operate globally, with just a tiny physical footprint in London; a story which illustrates how self-employed professionals, or small business owners, can expand geographic reach, and straddle multiple occupations.

Vineet Nayyar, the vice chairman of IT services company, Tech Mahindra, is agile in both literal and metaphorical ways: in his ability to exercise and stay fit, and in his ability to lead the acquisition and turnaround of Satyam Computer Services, through what could be called the 'architecture of rejuvenation'. His workplace reflects how agile thinking manifests itself through nimble business decisions and energized workplace design.

LYNDA GRATTON

Meeting place: Gratton can interact with clients in the common room at Somerset House

THE GLOBAL MICRO-ENTREPRENEUR

A tiny 100 sq. ft workplace, situated in one of Europe's most beautiful buildings, has caught my attention for many reasons. It is the office of Lynda Gratton and her cutting-edge research company, the Hot Spots Movement, located in Somerset House, a landmark property on London's historic Strand avenue.

Gratton is a management academic at the London Business School and a writer, and her company, the Hot Spots Movement, offers an unusual blend of research and consulting. She is the CEO of what I call a 'global micro-enterprise'–a small company (Hot Spots has less than ten employees) which is indisputably global in the scope of its operations. I am keen to understand whether the CEO of such a company employs entirely different work practices from her counterparts in larger organizations.

Perhaps even more importantly, I am visiting the compact workplace because it holds the key to a subject that affects all of us–the future of work.

This is the subject of Gratton's latest book, *The Shift: The Future of Work*

Is Already Here (2011), and the current research endeavour of the Hot Spots Movement. *The Shift* examines ways in which knowledge-based work will change in the coming decade, and offers individuals advice on future-proofing themselves and their careers. The author's personal work style, and her office space, bring some of her ideas to life.

She is the CEO of what I call a 'global micro-enterprise'–a small company (Hot Spots has less than ten employees) which is indisputably global in the scope of its operations.

Historic building, futuristic enterprise

Somerset House is the 'world's first civil services office block', says Mark Hislop, commercial director of the property. It was built in 1780 to house several departments of the British government, which continued to occupy it for nearly 200 years. Over the last decade, a prescient government decided to leverage its central London location and impressive architecture, and transformed it into a cultural and creative hub. This change of purpose resulted in leasing some existing office space to small companies with sizeable intellectual capital.

The Hot Spots office is basic in form, yet efficient in function. Six chairs and desks are placed against its white walls. A rectangular, centrally placed table with hinged flaps doubles as a meeting table. Large Mac desktops dominate the desks, and enable recurring Skype conversations between team members (one of whom is based in Singapore). An old-fashioned blackboard records names and travel dates.

Gratton herself has an assigned desk, which is the same as everyone else's, although she says she 'never works off it', and prefers having discussions over the meeting table, or reviewing work with colleagues on their computers, whenever she's in the office.

Where the office differs from most other corpo-

Common ground: Lynda Gratton prefers to have discussions with colleagues at the centrally placed table in her office

rate offices is the heritage facility's many shared spaces. Gratton can brainstorm with colleagues and visitors in a collegiate common room at the end of the corridor (where we have our conversation), or at the riverside terrace or the benches in the sprawling, statue-filled courtyard. The spaces are beautiful and inspiring, far removed from most corporate settings, a deliberate choice by Gratton. 'We chose them . . . offices can take the life out of you,' she states, 'but the physical environment is really conducive to the quality of work.'

'Offices can take the life out of you but the physical environment is really conducive to the quality of work.'

The choice of location is also strategic. Somerset House's other tenants are all highly innovative micro-enterprises, straddling public policy think tanks, media and design companies. Common spaces and an open-door policy encourage idea osmosis between companies, essential for any intellectually driven enterprise. 'We're beginning to understand that people learn from each other because they bump into each other in physical space,' explains Gratton. The small, cellular nature of the offices in Somerset House works 'brilliantly' for such specialized micro-enterprises such as Hot Spots, explains Hislop. Gratton agrees that the work atmosphere would have been entirely different in 'some horrible serviced

Over the last decade, Somerset House has been transformed into a cultural and creative hub

office, somewhere else'.

Location and setting are clearly critical to the success of Gratton's global micro-enterprise. In India, such settings exist for large technology companies (software parks), as well as some small and medium enterprises (many converted industrial units, for example). However, a government-backed 'creative quarter', designed specifically to ignite innovation, an essential element of economic competitiveness, is missing.

The future of work

A few traits define Gratton's work style, and are reflected in her workplaces. Foremost among these is the emphasis on flexibility. Gratton is an archetype 'portfolio careerist'; she is a writer and researcher, a full-time professor at the London Business School, a highly sought-after motivational speaker and a small-business owner.

Her multiple workplaces reflect her many avatars. Apart from the Somerset House lease, she has a dedicated office at the business school in Regent's Park. She writes from her home, in nearby Primrose Hill, as well as her weekend home in Sitges,

'I do most of my emails on my iPhone when I wake up in the morning. I don't spend any of my time during the day doing emails at all. That's actually a very good discipline.'

a seaside resort an hour away from Barcelona. 'I need complete silence when I write,' she declares.

Although her work hours and setting are extremely flexible, her work day 'is very, very structured. My diary is done till the end of the year,' she says. This means that she is free to organize her schedule and allocate time between teaching, writing, researching, speaking and advising. Even though she is not bound to a regimented routine of turning up at the same workplace every day, her calendar is extremely organized, so that she can productively combine all her pursuits.

In any given week, she may conduct a workshop with a client, speak at a conference, be on a jury and work on her books. Combining flexibility and discipline is not always easy for most knowledge workers, but research shows that flexibility significantly enhances individual productivity, she explains.

Second, she operates both virtually and globally. Her virtual footprint surpasses her physical footprint–she has assembled a global research consortium of twenty-seven organizations from around the world, such as British Telecom, the Singaporean government, and closer to home, Mahindra and Mahindra and Tata Consultancy Services. Unlike other consulting firms, Hot Spots collaborates virtually with its clients via a specially developed Web portal for its research. Fieldwork takes place online via conversations, as well as through face-to-face events and workshops.

Third, she is 'completely wired', yet extremely focused in her reliance on technology. She carries an iPhone and a Mac Air, has a large Macintosh at home, and has wireless Internet connectivity in all office locations. But she refrains from incessantly checking email during the day. 'I do most of my emails on my iPhone when I wake up in the morning. I don't spend any of my time during the day doing emails at all. That's actually a very good discipline,' she argues.

'Organizations must stop confusing hours worked with output, and must understand that people must not be chained to a desk to be productive.'

Finally, her area of interest is highly specialized and she is considered a global authority in the areas of human resources and organizational behaviour.

While organizations profess to offer these characteristics–flexibility, virtual collaboration, appropriate use of technology, global reach, razor-like focus, deep specialization and an inspiring work setting–the reality is that most knowledge workers are still bound to their desks in bland offices, answering emails or attending long meetings, with inadequate technology and tools for cross-functional collaboration. Most CEOs still occupy a corner suite, tucked away from the trenches, and like to jump on to aircraft for meetings.

Yet Gratton argues that her work style is possibly replicable. 'It is an organizational challenge more than an individual challenge. Organizations must stop confusing hours worked with output, and must understand that people must not be chained to a desk to be productive.' Certainly a rallying cry for the future.

23 October 2011

UPDATE: *Hot Spots has moved to a larger office within Somerset House. Gratton's latest book, The Key: How Corporations Succeed By Solving The World's Toughest Problems, came out in mid-2014.*

SUBROTO BAGCHI

Subroto Bagchi (right) holds a meeting in his office, which is also a common conference room

THE NOMADIC STORYTELLER

Subroto Bagchi's office is a conference room with a fabulous view of blue skies and palm trees. It is generously sized, as one might expect for the vice chairman of a well-known IT company such as Mindtree, situated on a sixteen-acre campus on the outskirts of Bangalore.

However, the conference room is a shared facility–open to any company employee. Bagchi says he 'gets right of first refusal' on its use, and others are free to occupy it when 'he's not around'–he travels for half the month (the company does have several other conference rooms).

Blue skies and palm trees lend context to Mindtree's 'living logo'–an arch that frames a live tree to form the stylized 'M' if viewed full on

Bagchi has occupied this space since he stepped down from his earlier role as chief operating officer (which he held till 2008) to become Mindtree's Gardener. As Gardener, his principal occupation is to 'huddle' with the company's 100 leaders, individually and in groups, to analyse, reflect, brainstorm–for what he terms 'sense-making'.

The office–dominated by a doughnut-shaped meeting table, off which Bagchi works–has little of the paraphernalia associated with a senior executive. When I met him, his collection of photographs and paintings was stacked against the wall. Though he plans to modify and personalize the room, he does not seem to be in a hurry to do so. At the moment, the room is entirely plug-and-play: a semi-transitional space, distinctly connected with the outdoors, both aspects that Bagchi says he values above all in his workplace.

'We're a fractal company; we're about distributed leadership.'

Natural growth and change

Bagchi traces these curious preferences to his childhood, narrating the almost mythical story of his early years in Orissa's tribal belts as the son of a government employee, shuffling between government quarters. These formative experiences, he says, led him to value 'harmony with nature' and 'not build attachment to any one physical space'. The nomadic existence continues: 'In my whole life, I have never lived in a house for three years non-stop and never used the same office for more than eighteen months,' says Bagchi.

Yet the office reveals more than a peripatetic nature. The choice of location was strategic. Mindtree's executive chairman Ashok Soota sits in another building on the same campus and Bagchi wanted to occupy a different wing in order to 'underline the fact that we're a fractal company; we're about distributed leadership'.

Such phrases point to Bagchi's layered thinking and multifaceted persona, as a popular blogger, writer, columnist, management philosopher and storyteller.

Space for a company's culture

Bagchi has an instinct for distilling management truths. Our conversation is peppered with his

A mural of sunflowers by children from the Spastics Society of Karnataka brightens one of the internal corridors

double-barrelled predictions on the future of the company.

'The postmodern organization will take advantage of a company's non-structure.'

'Increasingly, a corporation's relationship with its shareholders, customers and employees will be subscription-led.'

'Space is the enabler of our intellectual infrastructure and reflection of our emotional infrastructure.'

'The postmodern organization understands the power of feeling as an enabler of creation of economic value.'

These phrases reflect Bagchi's preoccupation with the changing relationships between employers, employees and their leaders in a competitive, dynamic world. Interestingly for me, this concern extends to physical spaces.

Mindtree is unique in its ability to articulate a connection between physical spaces and intellectual assets, which it believes is the key to its success as a knowledge enterprise. For Bagchi, 'space is the enabler of our intellectual infrastructure and reflection of our emotional infrastructure.' To him, spaces and buildings are not just standalone assets, but deeply integrated elements of a company's basic fabric, which affect and reflect its culture.

Mindtree's corridors and workspaces narrate a story about its origins and its identity.

Mindtree's management (including Bagchi) and its preferred architects Chandavarkar and Thacker, work closely to craft a distinctly 'Mindtree' campus experience. Just as Bagchi's own space highlights his itinerant nature and his desire for greenery, Mindtree's corridors and workspaces narrate a story about its origins and its identity.

Space as a narrative medium

The metaphor of nature is visible throughout the campus. New recruits are first assigned to the 'Orchard', a suite of common rooms and classrooms. Visitors to the campus are received not by art, but a 'living logo'–a tree framed to form an 'M'. A stylized metal tree grows next to the reception. Training programmes take place in the 'Rainforest'. Employees take a coffee break in 'pods'.

Walking through the facility, I experience the power of space as a narrative medium. This approach ties back into the other compelling aspect of Bagchi's personality: his storytelling abilities. Readers of his books will testify to his anecdotal skills. Our conversation is laced with stories–with lessons from seafaring salmon and coconut trees–just as much as it is lined with management truths.

Mindtree is an unusual example of corporate design evangelism, and I wonder about the impact on business, if any. Just over a decade old, Mindtree declared revenue of ₹ 1296 crores in 2009-10–sizeable, but far from top-tier. Yet in terms of corporate image and presence, it certainly punches above its weight.

Spaces and buildings are not just standalone assets, but deeply integrated elements of a company's basic fabric, which affect and reflect its culture.

Perhaps that's exactly what Bagchi means when he says the goal is to create a 'memorable' company. His office, and the lush Mindtree campus, are not easily forgotten.

15 June 2010

UPDATE: *Ashok Soota resigned from Mindtree in January 2011. Subroto Bagchi has been chairman of Mindtree since April 2012.*

Nayyar's corner office has a fantastic view of the Sahyadri hills

VINEET NAYYAR

THE YOUTHFUL VETERAN

I come across something quite unexpected in my guided tour of the senior management enclave of the Tech Mahindra corporate office in Hinjewadi, outside Pune: a gym. With a treadmill, stepper and weights machine, it is compact in footprint, yet highly efficient, quite like the IT services company's vice chairman, managing director and chief executive officer, Vineet Nayyar.

Nayyar says he exercises daily, at 6.00 a.m. at home or around lunchtime in the office. 'It is almost a condition of my employment. Even when I was moving to Tech Mahindra's (Mumbai office) in 2005, the first thing I did was set up a gym next to my office.'

The made-in-India kettle is one of the few personal items in his office.

While many companies have a gym or the odd treadmill and weight training equipment somewhere within their premises, this is the first time I have encountered a gym at such close proximity to top management's personal quarters. Nayyar says it is used regularly by his immediate colleagues and him, jokingly adding that exercising is a good way to conduct meetings. 'Whoever gets

'It is almost a condition of my employment. Even when I was moving to Tech Mahindra's (Mumbai office) in 2005, the first thing I did was set up a gym next to my office.'

off the cardio machines first loses the debate,' he laughs.

Architecture of rejuvenation

Much has been written about Nayyar and his avatars as bureaucrat and chief executive, with diverse organizations such as the Haryana government, the World Bank, GAIL (India), HCL and now, Tech Mahindra and its subsidiary Mahindra Satyam.

Nayyar and his team have been credited with turning around a flailing Mahindra Satyam in under three years. I am visiting him with a more specific agenda: to understand this 'architecture of rejuvenation', to really be a part of this secret of turning around Mahindra Satyam, a company most people had written off.

Tech Mahindra bought Satyam Computer Services Ltd in April 2009, renaming it Mahindra Satyam. Nayyar, along with senior colleagues, began managing Mahindra Satyam as an independent business, taking on the additional role of chairman of Mahindra Satyam. The company made a loss in fiscal 2009, but turned the corner by fiscal 2010.

Although Mahindra Satyam's campuses are not in the same cities as Tech Mahindra's, Nayyar asks me to meet him in Tech Mahindra's Hinjewadi campus. It is one he was personally involved in constructing, and he feels it best captures his work style. Mahindra Satyam campuses were all built by Satyam's founder B. Ramalinga Raju, he tells me, adding that both companies, and their facilities, will be integrated in the future.

Room with a view

Nayyar's cabin itself is functional, furnished with only the essentials of corporate life: a desk, a

Nayyar says that besides keeping him fit, the gym is also a great place for team meetings

chair, a sofa, armchairs, a coffee table and an obligatory painting, none of which appear to be exceptionally expensive. The only personal item of any significance in Nayyar's cabin is a 'nicely designed' kettle which he noticed was made in India. He adds, 'I must say that normally Indian products are not known for their design.'

The executive suite is a self-contained unit, located in the same building as other work areas. Apart from cabins for the six senior management members, there is a boardroom, two meeting rooms (one with video facilities), a lunch room, support staff seating and the gym. While most corporate suites have similar facilities, this particular office layout appears to encourage physical integration between its occupants; vital in promoting collaboration. The cabins are linked together in a U-shaped format and the layout of the common areas and cabins is such that people end up running into each other all the time.

The cabins are linked together in a U-shaped format and the layout of the common areas and cabins is such that people end up running into each other all the time.

Pace and teamwork

These physical aspects of the workspace are a subtle reflection of three aspects of Nayyar's working style. First, the proximity to the gym and his regular habit of exercising highlights his stamina, clearly critical to maintaining pace and

'My senior guys have all been with me for fifteen years. We all started in a one-room shop in HCL and we grew.'

dynamism. Nayyar professes that his one-hour exercise routine has been a daily practice for more than two decades as 'it gives higher energy. If you don't do it, you start drooping, especially as you get older.'

The second notable aspect is teamwork. Nayyar repeatedly emphasizes the role of Tech Mahindra's corporate team. 'My senior guys have all been with me for fifteen years. We all started in a one-room shop in HCL and we grew,' he affirms–a long innings for any team in any industry. 'Personal friendship and an amazing amount of equality' drives the team, he says, characterizing the group's work style as a 'panchayat'. 'The great thing is we have a lot of fun. If you come to our meetings no one will take us seriously at all, we're laughing most of the time,' Nayyar claims. C.P. Gurnani, CEO of Mahindra Satyam, and Nayyar's colleague for the last fifteen years, clarifies that 'we are not about competing with each other or even with others, we like to think we are building this together, which means having fun.'

The third most obvious aspect of Nayyar's workspace and work style is his ability to prioritize 'functionality' over 'ostentation'. This is a deliberate choice, as it is both a personal and corporate value. 'You don't want your clients coming here and saying, "my God this is what I've been paying money for" he smiles. It's also a practical approach, since Nayyar has several offices in Hyderabad, Mumbai and Delhi and regularly operates from them.

Form, function, focus

These values are as visible on the rest of the twenty-five-acre, purpose-built campus, completed in December 2009. Nayyar was involved in site selection, design brief and execution, insisting on 'aesthetics, use of natural stone, use of permanent materials for easy maintenance, and ample daylight'. The resulting campus is functional, yet visually pleasing and employee-oriented, with comfortable, well-lit workspaces, landscaped breakout areas for its 8000 staffers to mingle, and amenities such as a dedicated training floor, big food court, library and college-style amphitheatre.

'The great thing is we have a lot of fun. If you come to our meetings no one will take us seriously at all, we're laughing most of the time.'

Knowing what to prioritize, and how to extract the most bang for the buck are two personality traits that Nayyar seems to have employed in the Satyam turnaround. The first year was devoted to 'surviving the near-death experience', he says, by settling liabilities, eliminating unnecessary real estate, addressing legal cases, reassuring clients and managing workforce attrition. The second year was spent on 'making institutional reform, setting the finance systems right, putting in an enterprise resource planning system which worked'. The last six months have been about 'going back to customers, ensuring delivery and bringing back profitability'.

Energy, teamwork and functional focus, wrapped in a sense of humour: the key elements of a turnaround, expressed in the 'architecture of rejuvenation'. The script sounds easier than the execution.

27 November 2011

UPDATE: *Vineet Nayyar has been executive vice chairman and C.P. Gurnani has been managing director of the company since August 2012.*

COLLABORATION

WORKSTYLE

The hardest tasks usually sound the simplest. For example, getting people to work together is a fundamental challenge in business management. John Kotter, leadership guru and author, in a pivotal article in *What leaders really do* (1990) in the *Harvard Business Review* pointed out that 'a central feature of modern organizations is interdependence, where no one person has complete autonomy, where most employees are tied to many others by their work, technology, management systems and hierarchy. These linkages present a special challenge when organizations attempt to change.

Unless many individuals line up and move together in the same direction, people will tend to fall all over one another. What executives need to do, however, is not organize people, but align them . . . which means communicating the new direction to those who can create coalitions that understand the vision and are committed to its achievement.'

Alignment, collaboration and getting employees to work together are basic premises underlying contemporary open-plan workplace design, but implementation remains contentious. A growing body of research points out that open-plan offices can be unproductive for employees, due to noise, distractions, constant interruptions and lack of privacy. Researchers increasingly suggest that companies should provide employees with opportunities for private work as well as collaborative work.

So it was interesting to understand why, and how, some chief executives were facilitating more collaborative working in their companies. For example, Shikha Sharma, the managing director of Axis Bank, when moving to a new corporate headquarters, used architectural scale to reinforce a message about flattened hierarchies, in her C-suite, as well as across the bank.

Shantanu Khosla, chief executive of Procter and Gamble's Indian operations, gave up his private office altogether, and sat at a workstation alongside his peers. Aruna Jayanthi of Capgemini, a global IT company, believes in using technology to build interpersonal relationships. These are clear signs of top-down organizational change, using workplaces, technologies and processes as tools.

Aruna Jayanthi has a classic IT office with a workstation for private work, and a round meeting table for discussions

ARUNA JAYANTHI

THE SOCIABLE TECHIE

A distinct sense of déjà vu accompanies me to the office of Aruna Jayanthi, chief executive officer of the Indian operations of Capgemini, a global technology, consulting and outsourcing firm. I'm meeting Jayanthi for the first time but as soon as I enter her private office, I know I've seen this type of cabin on dozens of occasions in the past. Situated within the Godrej business park in Mumbai's Vikhroli suburb, Jayanthi's cabin is a perfect template for the thousands of information technology (IT) offices that redefined Indian corporate interiors from the early 1990s.

It has a corner workstation for private work, a round meeting table for discussions, pin boards, shelves and cabinets. Compact, collaborative and computer-oriented, it differs from an earlier generation of senior management offices, which were more hierarchical, formal, larger and less tech-friendly, with a presidential, L-shaped desk, extensive storage, and sofas–this format continues to prevail in many chief executive suites to this day. The cabin is one among a line of private offices, not visibly

A miniature house from Holland, gifted by a visitor

'Our differentiation as a company is not from technology, it's from the application of technology to the customer, it's more the human aspects of understanding the customer.'

different from those of her colleagues, situated on the periphery of the floor.

There is a small selection of books, ranging from technology to leadership and management. A few personal mementoes decorate the office: photographs, gifts from global customers, leadership awards from business associations, and a particularly interesting miniature houseboat, from an internal team event in Kumarakom in Kerala. 'We gave each person a houseboat, and each man a lungi. Every man had to wear the lungi to the evening dinner, no excuses. And they all did, nearly 100 of them,' Jayanthi recalls with a chuckle.

It's all about people

Jayanthi's mementoes reinforce my personal belief that technology companies are essentially about people, not technology. The objects in her cabin suggest that the value lies in the relationships she has built–with her colleagues, customers and the wider business community–rather than in any technological wizardry.

Jayanthi agrees with my assessment. 'Our differentiation as a company is not from technology, it's from the application of technology to the customer, it's more the human aspects of understanding the customer. Am I willing to listen to his problem? It's not about writing the best program in the world. If it doesn't solve the customer's problem, it's the worst program in the world, in that sense,' she explains.

Although technology should work for people, it can also take over our lives. So how should we leverage it, without being dominated by it? My conversation with Jayanthi led me to draw a few conclusions about mastering technology at the workplace.

Efficient collaboration

Collaboration is one of the primary benefits of any workplace technology, such as email, conference call or videoconferencing. Jayanthi relies heavily on videoconferencing–'two-three times a day'–and says she has built-in videoconferencing facilities on her laptop, which she can access when she's travelling.

'If I want a team meeting, I just say, let's get together by video. I have almost stopped conference calls that are the norm in the IT industry.'

Group discussions over videoconference help develop consensus and ownership on a particular issue, she says. 'Often, even if I have already decided what it is, I might not talk about it, because then it comes like a top-down decision. You want the buy-in, you want the people to recognize that it is their decision,' she adds.

She prefers videoconferencing, rather than conference calls, because it leads to better decision-making and less 'free-riding', i.e., plugging into conference calls without really listening or contributing. 'If I want a team meeting, I just say, let's get together by video. I have almost stopped conference calls that are the norm in the IT industry. With conference calls, sometimes you only need a fifteen-minute meeting but people block time in chunks of one hour. Or people just switch off during conference calls, unlike video,' she observes.

Similarly, email is a good tool for communicating decisions, but not for conducting debates. 'Everyone replies with their opinion, you lose the thread and it becomes painful. Videoconference is good because you can drive decisions, drive a collaborative consensus and then share those decisions over email,' she says.

Another gift, of a postman from Sweden Post

Brainstorming via crowdsourcing

Jayanthi encourages idea-generation through crowdsourcing. 'I just love the whole concept of

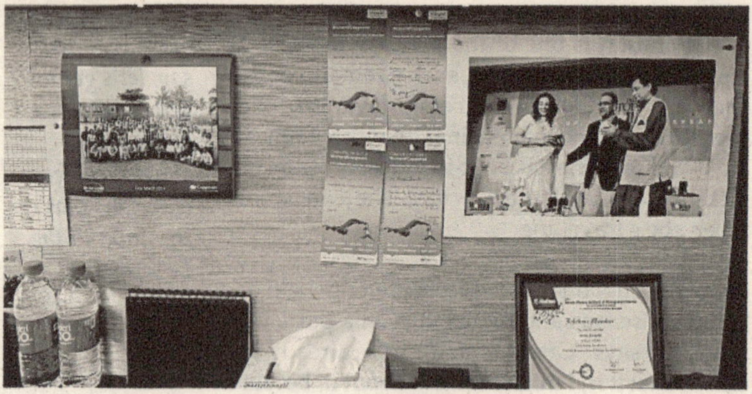

Awards and photographs dot Jayanthi's pin board and desk

crowdsourcing. If there's a problem, why should I assume that I have all the answers or the next level has all the answers?' she points out.

Two years ago, the company developed a crowdsourcing platform for idea exchange, open to all its employees, 40,000 at the time. 'Of the 5000-6000 replies generated, 90 per cent were junk. But some were so good, and one of them saved us months of effort in our way of doing annual appraisals,' she says.

'Are you able to really get a cohesive insight by looking at multiple pieces? And that to me is really the value when you start talking about big data.'

Big data: insight among the noise

Big data continues to be a buzzword, but discussion has generally triumphed over clarity. For Jayanthi, big data entails not losing sight of the forest for the trees; in other words, finding insight in the midst of noise.

'Are you able to really get a cohesive insight by looking at multiple pieces? And that to me is really the value when you start talking about big data. It's really looking at the numerical data, but more importantly we look at all the other stuff surrounding it–the softer factor, what are people saying about you in social media, in order to arrive at insight and identify future trends one can act on.'

She cites an example of a recent project for an Australian client where the company wanted to leverage social media. Jayanthi's team did some research online and identified a particular blogger who frequently marketed the company's services on various social media and other sites, and had his own following, whom the client was unaware of.

'These are the sort of customers and insights one can identify through big data. At the end of the day, you need to be able to relate to all the noise around, and use data either for driving more sales or bringing more efficiency in operations. Eventually it has to relate to something in the business,' Jayanthi points out.

Her views sparked an idea. While companies struggle with big data, like many of us, I struggle with the 'little data': family photographs and videos, stored on various devices, sometimes sorted and classified but not always viewed regularly. Maybe I should review and find personal insights–for example, all the first moments of early childhood. It will definitely be of more value than lots of individual pieces of data.

9 November 2014

Shantanu Khosla of Procter & Gamble works from an open-plan workstation, alongside his colleagues

SHANTANU KHOSLA

THE OPEN-OFFICE MAVERICK

The private office of Shantanu Khosla is notable for its absence: it doesn't exist. The managing director of Procter and Gamble's (P&G's) Indian operations has no chamber, or even a corner wall, to himself. He sits at a 6x6 ft workstation, surrounded by co-workers and a product showcase that currently displays diapers, in an entirely open-plan layout.

If he wants a change of scenery, he can choose the closest available armchair from those lining the office's full-length glass windows. If he wishes to conduct a meeting, he can book himself into one of the facility's many 'huddle rooms'–none are especially reserved for him. If a colleague would like to speak with him, she can simply saunter up to his desk for a quick conversation. At lunchtime, he dines in the company cafeteria, where he is free to make himself a machine-brewed cup of coffee.

Egalitarian, informal and exposed, Khosla's workspace is undoubtedly the boldest attempt at flattening workplace hierarchies in an organization in India that I have personally experienced. Given P&G's respectable girth in India–350 people in its Mumbai headquarters, and revenue of just over $800 million (₹ 3648 crores) for the year ended June 2010–it provokes further scrutiny.

'You have to adjust behaviours to get the most out of (open offices). You can't just say I'm going to tear down the walls and it's going to be open. It all has to come together.'

A new work culture

Khosla attributes the radical design to a decade-old P&G global policy, which initiated a company-wide migration to open offices. 'What we did then is what you see a lot of people who talk about open offices now actually doing–which means that senior executives are not really in cabins but in open offices,' he says. Over time, even senior managers at P&G were plucked out from their cabins. Khosla states that 'now we're pretty much like this everywhere, including Cincinnati', the American Midwestern location of the mother ship.

'This' means a complete embargo on individual private offices, an increased square foot allocation towards public spaces, meeting rooms and employee amenities, a significant investment in supporting infrastructure and a transformed work culture, which eliminates any level-linked perks, such as reserved parking slots, separate dining spaces or different-sized workstations or seating.

Khosla emphasizes the need to connect a new workplace to a new work culture, explaining 'you have to adjust behaviours to get the most out of it. You can't just say I'm going to tear down the walls and it's going to be open. It all has to come together.' Improved telecommunication systems, such as wireless networks, laptops and networked printers, are essential to unshackle employees from their cubicles. 'Cultural interventions are equally vital', he says, as 'people have to want to work in teams, people have to feel comfortable; that's the way to get stuff done.'

There appears to be little dispute on the benefits. Greater visibility demystifies senior management

Khosla conducts his meeting anywhere on the premise, like this one in the cafeteria

and results in faster decision-making. 'If you were to walk around our office, you couldn't tell who was vice president, or who was a secretary,' notes Khosla, as he pauses by a colleague's workstation for a brief exchange. Greater proximity between team members results in more collaboration, particularly between cross-functional teams. Khosla points to the organic, non-linear layout of the workstations, which explicitly encourages employees to manoeuvre and circulate among their team-based clusters, as they walk to and from their desks.

'If you were to walk around our office, you couldn't tell who was vice president, or who was a secretary.'

The open-plan office is one element in a progressive workplace policy, the other being a clearly articulated work-from-home policy, initiated in India in keeping with global trends. Four years ago, the company allowed employees to work from home, up to two days a week, equipping them with a broadband connection and ergonomic furniture in their residences. Almost one third of its workforce follows this practice regularly, Khosla tells me.

Maverick techie

Khosla's gadget-friendly disposition reinforces open-plan working; he clearly follows the 'work is what you do, not where you are' philosophy.

Khosla likes to work from an airport-style meeting table next to his desk

While he maintains a nine-to-six schedule in the office, he is 'always working, 24/7. It normally takes me thirty seconds to reply to an email. I clear it as it comes.' His desk is as uncluttered as his email inbox, with no signs of personal attachment to physical location.

We found him reading off an iPad on an armchair–'a wonderful device'–which he says he's been using for email for six months, and has almost replaced his laptop ('I haven't travelled with a laptop for a long time now.') Magazines and newspapers are read on both iPad and iPhone; his only hard copy print subscription is a daily newspaper. Regular videoconferencing with overseas colleagues has substituted frequent travel. A P&G veteran, having worked in offices of various dimensions, in Newcastle, Kobe, Singapore and Kuala Lumpur, he is adamant that he 'doesn't miss his cabin at all'.

Workplace innovation

The approach is not easily replicable. Our conversation confirms my belief that the most successful office fit-outs are those where top management views them as opportunities for organizational behavioural change, and ensures that human resources policies, corporate culture and physical

'I am always working, 24x7. It normally takes me thirty seconds to reply to an email. I clear it as it comes.'

infrastructure are all equally aligned with the company's square-foot growth. Most of the time, though, a new or renovated office space is viewed merely as an operational, real estate project–the necessary outcome of headcount expansion or reduction.

P&G's innovation-led business philosophy, one of the consumer product behemoth's most enduring traits, also makes it a likely candidate for embracing alternative approaches to workplace design.

The latest experiment in India is 'hotdesking', a practice where 'teams have dedicated spaces, but the individual doesn't have a space', Khosla informs me. Team members will share desks, depending on travel and work-from-home schedules, for greater spatial efficiency. Perhaps, when I next visit, Khosla's dedicated workstation itself might have disappeared.

29 November 2010

UPDATE: *Shantanu Khosla resigned from P&G in May 2015.*

CEO Shikha Sharma's office space is compact and is divided into two sections–her personal space and a meeting room

SHIKHA SHARMA

THE UNDERSTATED RADICAL

The corner office on the eighth floor of Axis Bank's new corporate office in Worli, Mumbai, doesn't appear particularly radical. Less than 200 sq. ft in area, it is small, with just enough space for a desk, a round discussion table, a few chairs and a cabinet. The office space is spare, decorated only with the obligatory family photographs, Ganesha idols, a few books, commemorative plates and artefacts. Its inhabitant is Shikha Sharma, the managing director and CEO of Axis Bank, India's third largest private bank. The understated aesthetics reinforce my perception of Sharma as a quiet, soft-spoken business leader who believes 'that you don't talk (about an accomplishment) before you've done it'.

Ganesha idols dot her private cabin

Next to her private cabin is an equally compact, lounge-style meeting room, with eight armchairs and a coffee table, for informal interactions with visitors. The decision to bifurcate her workspace into personal and public spheres also reflects her reserved personality. 'For me, my workspace is my personal space where I work and I deal with small teams, and I don't necessarily want clients to come

'For me, my workspace is my personal space where I work and I deal with small teams, and I don't necessarily want clients to come into my personal workspace.'

into my personal workspace,' she says.

Economies of scale

The management had planned to construct a new office building, but soon after joining the bank, Sharma realized 'that we didn't have the luxury to wait to build our own office because we were just too inefficiently structured physically'. Employees were strewn across thirteen premises in downtown Mumbai, which made meeting-and-greeting employees 'an absolute nightmare', says Sharma. So Axis Bank purchased an office building nearing completion in post-industrial Worli.

The office design follows global best practices in ways that few home-grown companies have the desire, or the courage, to emulate. The eight-storey building has an impressive footprint–each floor is 32,000-35,000 sq. ft. Managing such large-scale floor plates can be tricky; such offices often suffer from visual monotony, with unending rows of workstations, cabins and corridors.

Architecture firm Space Matrix responded to Sharma's brief of 'collaboration, flattened hierarchies and openness' by cleverly tackling the expansive scale. Cabins are placed away from windows, towards the central core of the building, so that natural light reaches more employees seated at open-plan workstations. Each floor has 'networking hubs'–essentially, open meeting areas–strategically placed between workstation zones to encourage communication between co-workers. A hefty 35 per cent of total square footage is devoted to common areas, and shared amenities include training rooms, a gym, library, canteen and terrace garden.

The interior fit-out budget has been devoted to employee welfare by giving them better furniture and more real estate, rather than investing in

The spaces that have been freed by keeping cabins compact have been devoted to common areas; staffers get more space for meetings and discussions

expensive works of art or interior finishes. The resulting workplace is more comfortable, although much more modest in appearance than its peers.

Sharma's own cabins, as well as those of her colleagues, seemingly reflect her ambitions for the bank, as well as her personality. The workplace is radical in its subtle approach to scale: Architectural scale has been used to reinforce a management message.

The workplace is radical in its subtle approach to scale: Architectural scale has been used to reinforce a management message.

Scale is a fascinating word because it is one of the few technical terms to straddle the language of business and the language of architecture. CEOs and architects usually have entirely different concerns, and employ entirely different vocabularies. But the concept of scale unites their thinking–physical, real estate scale can be a powerful expression of a company's economic scale (actual or desired).

Making the work flow

At Axis House, the office space in its totality is unusually egalitarian. All directors on the senior executive floor have equal, pocket-sized cabins, just marginally larger than those of their junior colleagues elsewhere in the building. All employees–regardless of stature–sit on the same

'We wanted same-sized cabins, with the same tables and chairs for everybody to demonstrate flatness and reduce the impact of hierarchy.'

ergonomic Liberty Chair by American manufacturer Humanscale. Priced at approximately ₹ 45,000, it is an expensive proposition by Indian standards to acquire for all staff members.

Such equality is rare in corporate hierarchies, especially in large organizations. For Sharma, it was a deliberate design principle. 'We wanted same-sized cabins, with the same tables and chairs for everybody to demonstrate flatness and reduce the impact of hierarchy,' she says.

Second, it is unusually sensible. The space freed up by keeping cabins compact has been devoted to common areas. A variety of different 'work settings' have been created by intelligently modulating the generous scale of the 10,500-sq. ft senior executive wing, facilitating different sorts of conversations between co-workers–formal and informal, structured and spontaneous.

There are three 'lounge meeting rooms', where Sharma and her colleagues can hold informal interactions, such as our conversation. Formal discussions which require presentations take place in 'structured' meeting rooms, as Sharma refers to them, or in the company boardroom.

For casual, spontaneous chats with colleagues or visitors, Sharma can choose one of the many clusters of chairs that are grouped, restaurant style, in the transition spaces between cabins and meeting rooms. Thus, there are four different 'work settings' just on one floor, all of which are equally open to Sharma and her colleagues.

The workflow-oriented layout reflects a senior manager's average working day: Sharma says her day is spent between 'meetings, presentations and travelling, not in her cabin'. The most appropriate design solution: a space-efficient, shared suite of meeting rooms, tailored for diverse discussions. The layout also promotes collaboration, meeting Sharma's stated goal of making the bank 'more team-oriented'.

Executive committee meetings have become 'deeper, intense and more open', she says, adding, 'It is very interesting how a simple physical change can make such a huge difference.'

Six months into the new office, Sharma notes its positive effects. Executive committee meetings have become 'deeper, intense and more open', she says, adding, 'It is very interesting how a simple physical change can make such a huge difference.'

Sharma states that her ambitions for the bank are 'to build on its strengths so we can continue to scale' and 'to create a great generation of leaders'. Her nuanced interpretation of scale, as judged by her office space, suggests she is on course to meet her goals.

19 June 2011

CRAFTSMANSHIP

On the face of it, the offices of Babasaheb Kalyani, Rajiv Bajaj and Ralf Speth look like any other corporate suite: spacious, private workplaces with desks and meeting tables. But each space tells a subtle story, which captures a common trait: a passion for automobile design, engineering and manufacturing, expressed in different ways.

Just outside Kalyani's office is a portrait of Ganesha, composed of the company's automotive parts, a tribute to divinity by metallurgy; one of the few chief executives to explicitly connect work and worship.

In a balcony adjoining Bajaj's cabin, there are wrought-iron chairs and tables, where he huddles with his team to create products; the only chief executive with this sort of arrangement in his workspace.

Only premium automobiles decorate Speth's office; he was also the only chief executive to test my design knowledge during the course of this series.

Their shared commitment to their products, and to the innovation, design and development process can be understood as a sign of craftsmanship, or the desire to do a job well for its own sake. This is a leadership trait that gets far too little attention, but to me is extremely important in terms of its impact on innovation.

Richard Sennett, eminent thinker and humanities professor at the London School of Economics, explores the notion of craftsmanship in the modern workplace in his book *The Craftsman* (2008). He believes that the values of the craftsman, rather than pure competition, will produce superior work in any modern industry: a provocative thesis for modern work life.

Babasaheb Kalyani's spacious office with its modest decor

BABASAHEB NEELKANTH KALYANI

THE MODERN-DAY ALCHEMIST

This is probably the largest executive office I've visited in the series to date–a six-seater meeting table, a huge desk, a sofa-seating area bigger than most living rooms and a large open door. The cabin's generous sprawl is a luxury that can only be bestowed by industrial plants (or public sector banks) on head honchos operating out of the headquarters.

In this case, I am in Pune to meet Babasaheb Neelkanth Kalyani, chairman and managing director, Bharat Forge Ltd, one of the world's largest manufacturers of metallurgical components. His suite is located in one of the several office blocks on the company's 100-acre campus, alongside dozens of manufacturing sheds and neatly parked scooters. The office block was built more than twenty years ago, he tells me, and it houses corporate functions such as sales, marketing, international business and legal. His son, Amit Kalyani, executive director, has an office on the same floor as Kalyani.

National and international certificates and citations line the walls of the conference room

'The office has been this way for a long time, I have an open-office culture, everyone can always walk in.'

Like many industrial peers, although the room is spacious, its decor is modest, consisting mainly of a Srinathji painting (given to Kalyani by a friend), a framed Padma Bhushan certificate awarded to Kalyani in May 2008, and a few scattered objects, mostly gifts or mementoes. There are no expensive paintings, rugs or gadgets, and the furniture looks quite seasoned. 'The office has been this way for a long time, I have an open-office culture, everyone can always walk in,' says Kalyani, pointing to the door which remains open during our conversation. The three work settings (private work, formal meeting table, informal meeting) are quite standard for chief executive suites.

Work is worship

Two specific objects really capture my attention. First, a Ganesh portrait consisting of a collage of metallurgical automotive components, placed at the entrance to the cabin. A portrait of Kalyani's father (the founder of the metal forgings business) is placed in front of the Ganesh portrait. The work is a tribute to divinity, paternity and prosperity, all united by metallurgy.

Second, a detailed list of operational and financial figures, pinned discreetly next to his desk; top-of-the-mind is not a familiar expression for me. for the occupant seated at the chairman's desk, but not visible to visitors. Both items capture Kalyani's reputation as a hands-on business leader, his zeal undiminished though he has been working in this field for over four decades–and I'll come back to their particular significance.

Speaking his mind

Kalyani is known to speak his mind, particularly on issues related to economic growth and manufacturing, and he is predictably blunt during our conversation. 'Two decades were lost in the Indian manufacturing sector by people trying to find partners as collaborators, joint venture partners and all that. What happened because of that is we became a slave-manufacturing nation. We didn't manufacture anything. We just became slaves to manufacturing,' he emphasizes.

'It took us twenty years to get to where we are. But in twenty years we went from zero to no. 1 in the world.'

He is equally matter-of-fact about how he bucked the trend. As Kalyani has often recounted to the media, from the late 1980s and early 1990s onwards, he decided to invest in expensive technology and automation, rather than hiring large numbers of relatively unqualified workers, in order to build technical capabilities. Today, the company's highly automated manufacturing plants and its skilled workforce are at the heart of its global competitiveness.

'It was a very painful process, and it took us twenty years to get to where we are. But in twenty years we went from zero to no. 1 in the world,' he says. 'We are a multinational company. About 40 per cent of our workforce is outside India and 70 per cent of our business is outside India in terms of sales . . . In the products that we supply, we have more than 50 per cent market share.'

An array of national and international certificates and citations line the walls of the conference room next door; appreciation of Kalyani's efforts in taking Bharat Forge overseas. 'I've a huge number of recognitions. I've received the highest civilian awards in Sweden, Germany, France,' he states.

Turning base metals into 'gold'

The tricky part of making metallurgical components such as automobile crankshafts is that it is both art and science, where accumulated knowledge, skills and expertise are as important as high-tech equipment. Hence, I use the term 'modern-day alchemist' for Kalyani–someone who uses contemporary technology, processes

'We are a multinational company. About 40 per cent of our workforce is outside India and 70 per cent of our business is outside India in terms of sales.'

and thinking to turn old-fashioned metal into cash. The Ganesh portrait highlights the extent to which Kalyani reveres his product (the research and development department is the only other area where the Ganesh portrait has been placed). Kalyani's passion for innovation is characteristic of a successful automotive chief executive. He is determined to create technology to drive his business, rather than adopt technology from elsewhere.

He speaks of innovation in terms of two tangible resources: human capital and digital technology; two areas that companies often struggle to integrate with business strategy, and which have not always featured in great detail in chief executive conversations in this series.

'There are almost 100 forging companies in Pune, but most of them don't have the ecosystem within them to create technology. By ecosystem, I mean the strong manufacturing capability. We have a total of 4000 people in this company, of which more than 2000 are engineers,' explains Kalyani.

Kalyani's detail orientation and commitment to innovation becomes apparent when he begins talking about how to create 'the manufacturing ecosystem within a company'. Most companies impart some training to new recruits. Kalyani decided to rewrite the syllabus, for both new recruits and existing employees, to improve productivity and capabilities.

The company partnered with several engineering schools to tailor-make curricula for its employees to enhance skills, productivity and individual self-esteem. These include a three-year, part-time engineering programme with the Birla Institute of Technology and Science (BITS) Pilani for its non-engineering workforce, an engineering business management programme with the UK's University of Warwick for middle- managers, and a master of technology programme for R&D scientists with the Indian Institute of Technology, Bombay, with special courses such as 'computational mathematics, advanced metallurgy-related courses, material science courses and those related to our business', says Kalyani.

'There are almost 100 forging companies in Pune but most of them don't have the ecosystem within them to create technology.'

The investments are paying off, he says. '40 per cent of our revenue now comes from areas other than automotive components. So it was an easy transition to move into new technologies because we had the ecosystem with flexible manufacturing platforms and teams that could work across industry verticals.'

He is equally committed to investing in digital technologies to propel the company's manufacturing capabilities. 'Technology is moving to additive manufacturing. It is moving to laser processing, it is moving to electron beams. Everything uses a very high level of basic metallurgical knowledge (without that you can't melt materials) and a very high level of computing knowledge. In five years we will have a factory with thirty to forty of these machines producing our parts,' he promises.

I look forward to visiting then.

25 August 2014

A portrait of Kalyani's father, the founder of the metal forgings business

RAJIV BAJAJ

Bajaj's office has several work- settings for private and group work

THE INTUITIVE JEWELLER

I am in a corner office, in a factory on the outskirts of Pune, at the head office of a plant I have visited several times since childhood, and my view of India's automobile industry is being altered rapidly. This is the office of Rajiv Bajaj, managing director of Bajaj Auto, one of India's largest two- and three-wheeler manufacturers.

I am not prone to gushing; I love nothing more than arguing with those in positions of immediate authority. Bajaj, who took over as MD in 2005, is the ideal candidate for an informed debate–a distant older brother figure, whose family have been our friends for decades, but equally, someone with whom I have rarely interacted, and indeed, never duelled.

His soccer talisman

I arrive at his office, fully prepared to cross-examine him on why he is hell-bent on sacrificing his father Rahul Bajaj's hard-earned market share in favour of selling just bikes, rather than all two-wheelers. My perception of Bajaj is of a committed manufacturing geek, an impassioned hobbyist at most.

But I'm in for a surprise. His office, and our hour-long discussion, confirm the gap between appearance and reality, and how important it is to be able to rapidly recalibrate perceptions of a person, and a company.

Bajaj huddles with his senior management team at a wrought iron table and chairs, on a balcony outside the office. 'This is where all our new products are created,' he says.

Five forces of strategy

Bajaj's cabin is meditative, controlled, elegant, detached and aligned: five words that summarize his personality, and his approach to work. There is visual evidence for each of these descriptors.

First, the room is quiet, calm and well- ventilated–the benefits of being located in a manufacturing plant as opposed to a city. Like many cabins of senior managers, it has three distinct work settings: a formal meeting space with a conference table where we conduct our interview, an informal sofa and coffee table for more casual chats, and a study table, deliberately placed against the wall, away from view, for thinking and writing. 'I don't want a visitor to be looking at my papers. It's not fair to me, not fair to him,' he remarks, explaining why he has chosen this position for the table.

There is also a fourth work setting: a wrought-iron table and chairs, on a balcony outside the office, where Bajaj huddles with his senior management team. 'This is where all our new products are created,' he says. The furniture lacks hierarchy, and is designed for a meeting of equals.

Second, the atmosphere is controlled and deliberate, just like Bajaj's strategy to focus only on bikes, rather than trying to grab market share wherever it is available. For example, a row of Ganapatis sit on a shelf, some with flowers in front, neatly placed as you would find on a Japanese manufacturing shop- floor. The desk features mementoes of his gurus, including B.K.S. Iyengar and the Japanese manufacturing expert Professor Yamaguchi.

The whiteboard offers insight into this thinking: 'Yoga is alignment–B.K.S. Iyengar.' 'Before we embark on the process of possibilities, we must start with the purity of principles.' Another one is more abstract: 'The centre is the mentor, it is the logic of magic.'

Bajaj is not the type to inscribe these for my benefit; the sayings reflect his deep understanding of yoga and homoeopathy, and his unique ability to apply them to business strategy, and to a manufacturing company in particular, in a systematic and rigorous manner (his philosophy and techniques comprise a separate conversation in itself).

Third, the space, which is a combination of art deco sofas and old-fashioned wood-panelling, combined with a cutting-edge black palette, comes across as elegant. It could be something straight out of Mad Men, the witty, cult American TV series set on Madison Avenue. 'The brief (to interior designer Darryl Lewis) was black, the brief was strong,' Bajaj summarizes. There is room for improvement in the finishes, which Bajaj acknowledges.

Fourth, Bajaj is clear that he wanted a study table facing the wall because he needs to be detached from the world around sometimes. 'In all my life, there are three things I've not done–I've never owned a suit, never relied on any market research and never worked on a computer. So I have to write everything. This is the way I turn myself away from the world,' he states.

'In all my life, there are three things I've not done–I've never owned a suit, never relied on any market research and never worked on a computer. So I have to write everything. This is the way I turn myself away from the world.'

Motorcycle artwork in the office

A large photographic print of a cabin in the Swiss wilderness by Mukesh Batra, Bajaj's preferred

A large photographic print of a cabin in the Swiss wilderness adds to the cabin's spacious feel

homoeopath and CEO of the homoeopathy chain Dr Batra's, is telling. To me the photograph captures Bajaj's reputation as a maverick and loner, someone who marches only to his own drumbeat.

Finally, the space is aligned (and given Bajaj's passion for yoga, it would be ironic if it wasn't). Everything is there for a reason, everything has its place, whether it's a painting of horses, his soccer talisman with the motto, 'When you control the ball, you control the score' (Pele), or family photographs, a statue of Nandi, the Hindu god Shiva's carrier, or mementoes of his gurus on the study table. The placement and location of furniture, books, artwork, whiteboard and personal accessories is cohesive.

The whiteboard offers insight into this thinking: 'Yoga is alignment–B.K.S. Iyengar.' 'Before we embark on the process of possibilities, we must start with the purity of principles.

Handcrafting a company

The intuitive jeweller label defines Bajaj well because he is clearly handcrafting his company, blending intuition with reason and logic, as many senior managers tend to do. He seeks mentors, and more importantly, listens to them. He crafts his own theories, and forges a way ahead for his team. The Bajaj version of automobile manufacturing, I'm beginning to realize, rests on the 'pursuit of perfection': control, alignment, elegance, detachment and calm.

More motorcycle-related memorabilia

To my mind, Bajaj's strategy of focusing on bikes enables the company to be as strong a brand, and as innovative a manufacturer, as Toyota, BMW or Honda, as long as it has its own distinctive positioning, purpose and personality. The name can easily travel the world. I believe the day is not far when he can ride his bike in the hills of Santa Monica, US, on Arabian highways, or in the bylanes of Shanghai, China. If I had to make a prediction, my bet would be on the dark horse.

3 February 2013

Speth describes each of the miniature models in his room in detail

RALF SPETH

THE PASSIONATE ENGINEER

The two-storeyed corporate headquarters I'm visiting is modest in all respects, except one: A fleet of Jaguar and Land Rover automobiles is parked in its forecourt, including the new Jaguar F-Type. I am in Coventry in the British Midlands to meet Ralf Speth, the chief executive officer of Jaguar Land Rover (JLR), and the man seen as responsible for leading the company's turnaround, after it was bought by Tata Motors in 2008.

'Product, product, product'

The fleet in front of the office block consists largely of company vehicles for senior management, I am told. The two brands continue to exert their presence inside the building, and inside Speth's glass-walled office, which is almost entirely bare of decorative accessories. Only a Jaguar painting on the wall and a few miniature models of specific Jaguar and Land Rover vehicles add vibrancy to the room–he describes each one in some detail.

A miniature Jaguar model in Speth's room

By now, I've realized that Speth is clearly more

'If we deliver a solid product, engineer it in a solid way, have a good design, then I am quite sure we can make good business.'

than a design enthusiast–he is the only chief executive I've met to test my knowledge in this sphere. Before we begin our conversation, he walks me around the office, shows me a series of iconic wall- clocks in the cafeteria, and asks me to name the designer. Luckily I know the answer–email me if you'd like to know.

Speth's L-shaped desk is conventional, with a shiny chrome frame that reflects the company's industrial character. Although the room is large enough to accommodate a six-seater meeting table and a storage cabinet with a TV, there is little difference between Speth's cabin and those of his senior colleagues next to him. 'The office was designed by our designers,' Speth says, in a distinctive German accent.

The spare, non-hierarchical room, with just premium automobiles on display, is entirely congruous with Speth's strategic drive to focus on 'product, product, product' and 'whatever it takes to come up with competitive vehicles, with a killer combination of design and engineering'. A seasoned automotive industry professional, fifty-seven-year-old Speth insists: 'The priority is not to shoot for financial figures or for volumes, the focus is on the products. If we deliver a solid product, engineer it in a solid way, have a good design, then I am quite sure we can make good business.'

The Range Rover sports utility vehicle

Engineering a turnaround

It is a business mantra that has served the company well, so far. Speth joined the company in February 2010, when it was beginning to show the first signs of profitability. Since then, new product launches and global market expansion have propelled annual sales and profits before tax to £ 15.8 billion (around ₹ 1.4 trillion) and £ 1.675 billion, respectively, for the year ending

There is a fleet of Jaguar and Land Rover cars parked in front of the office block, including the Jaguar F-Type

March 2013. The company is now regarded as a poster child of British manufacturing competitiveness.

Speth's obvious passion for industrial design conceals an equally critical aspect of his personality–the engineer's ability to deal with detail, especially in tweaking and refining business strategy, until there is smooth alignment between all moving parts.

This becomes evident when he discusses how the turnaround took place. 'We tried to do restructuring and growth simultaneously, to free up cash and to inject that money into new programmes,' he explains. 'You have to know how you do it, where you do it and when you can do it. We precisely define when and how much money to inject, to get the best results,' he adds.

'We tried to do restructuring and growth simultaneously, to free up cash and to inject that money into new programmes. You have to know how you do it, where you do it and when you can do it. We precisely define when and how much money to inject, to get the best results.'

Investment in new products was accompanied by significant new hires in manufacturing, to cope with increased demand and a greater presence in previously underdeveloped markets such as China, which is now nearly as large as Europe in terms of sales.

Moderating the scale, timing and choice of investment is particularly important for the company

Speth's glass-walled office has a six-seater meeting table and a storage cabinet with a TV, but there's little by way of decorative accessories

since its key competitors, including Mercedes, Audi and BMW, are significantly larger in volumes and revenue. 'Volkswagen profits are higher than our sales,' Speth points out. 'We have to decide what is the right innovation, the right technology, what is the right product portfolio, in an even more thoroughly thought through way, in order to make sure we can grow in a profitable and sustainable way,' he says.

Managing nationalities

Speth's job also includes managing alignment of a different sort. Jaguar Land Rover has an assortment of varied stakeholders–a distinctively British heritage, a largely British workforce, an Indian parent and global sales operations, with an expanding Chinese footprint.

Some of these are reflected in the building. Three framed certificates with the royal family's crest are placed in the building's foyer. These 'royal warrants' officially certify that Jaguar Land Rover is a supplier of motor vehicles to the Queen, the Duke of Edinburgh and the Prince of Wales, and explicitly cite Speth as the recipient of the warrant. 'We are the only (motor vehicle) company with three royal warrants,' Speth says.

Interestingly, the Tata brand is not particularly visible at the corporate headquarters. Speth says it was discussed internally, as well as with the Tatas, and the conclusion was to not display it, although he doesn't recall the reasons for the decision.

'It is a British company but the owner is Tata. Without Tata, JLR could not exist at all, it's as simple as that.'

His views on the Tata group are much less ambiguous. 'It is a British company but the owner is Tata. Without Tata, JLR could not exist at all, it's as simple as that,' he says. Speth points out that there is a dedicated office near his own for visiting Tata colleagues. He particularly admires the 'visionary approach' of the Tata group's chairman- emeritus Ratan Tata, and the group's 'mid- to long-term' business outlook, adding that he feels 'very well integrated into the Tata empire'.

More than nationality, Speth says he looks for 'competence and passion for the business, for cars and for our brands. We don't want to see our company being located in the cellar of the British heritage museum, being dead as a brand. We want to be alive. We want to sit at the high table of the premium car manufacturers around the world.' Enough of a mission to galvanize Speth to start his workday at 7.00 a.m., and continue working until after dinner.

21 July 2013

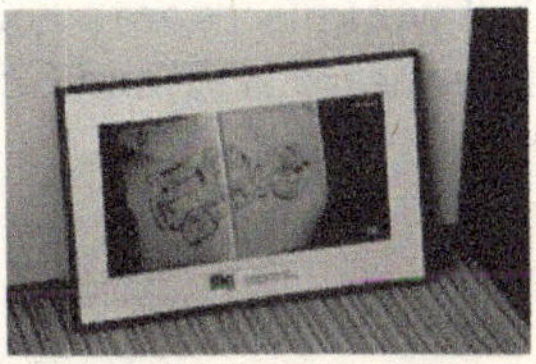

An advertising campaign for the Land Rover Defender

INTEGRATIVE THINKING

WORKSTYLE

No business leader lacks business strategy, but few have a well-articulated workplace strategy; most are unable to successfully integrate tangible and intangible assets. This can be attributed to what bestselling author, Daniel Pink, in his book *A Whole New Mind* (2005), describes as 'L-directed thinking', or 'a form of thinking which is characteristic of the left hemisphere of the brain'.

'The left hemisphere of the brain specializes in text, the right hemisphere specializes in context. The left hemisphere analyzes the details, the right hemisphere synthesizes the big picture. The left hemisphere is sequential, the right hemisphere is simultaneous,' he believes. In other words, L-directed thinking is 'sequential, literal, functional, textual and analytic' and 'R-directed thinking is simultaneous, metaphorical, aesthetic, contextual and synthetic'.

Martin Sorrell, the chief executive of global communications group WPP, differs from his peers in his ability to grasp both the creative potential, as well as the detailed costs, of his group's commercial real estate. Essentially, to integrate both ways of thinking.

Rajan Anandan, head of Internet services multinational Google's operations in India, similarly integrates both ways of thinking. In their book *How Google Works* (2014), authors Eric Schmidt and Jonathan Rosenberg describe this approach to working as examples of a 'smart creative' or someone who is 'business savvy, has technical knowledge, creative energy and a hands-on approach to getting things done'.

The benefits of this approach extend beyond workplaces, of course, but workplaces are a good starting point to understand some of the reasons for WPP and Google's commercial and creative success.

Martin Sorrell at a conference room in the WPP corporate office in London

MARTIN SORRELL

THE WORKPLACE STRATEGIST

Sir Martin Sorrell, the chief executive of WPP, is bending the cardinal rules of *Head Office* with characteristic Napoleonic authority. He will not permit even a peep into his private offices, as he prefers to guard his privacy. He merely deigns to admit that he is a 'big hoarder, with paraphernalia, such as the Superman suit my peers gave to me ten years ago'. So we meet him in a rather bland conference room, on the ground floor of the central London corporate offices of one of the world's largest advertising and marketing services groups.

Although we are denied the view from his own workplace, I am somewhat mollified when he shares his views on workplaces. Sorrell is the only CEO, in my experience, to have drawn a diagram of an office layout, and included it in the company's annual report, with a detailed description of its particular merits (page 27 of the agency's 1995 annual report has a diagram of the floor plan of a WPP agency in Buenos Aires, included alongside a note on the evolution of organization structures). Unlike many in his position, he has apparently dwelt on the relationship between workplaces and working styles, and has arrived at some conclusions on the business impact of architecture and design.

'In a business where our second biggest investment is property, it's important.'

Contradictory views

When you first hear him out, his views on the workplace appear contradictory.

The parent company WPP's own offices are remarkably low-key, but its member agencies operate from inspiring, often award-winning workplaces, which occupy more than 23.7 million sq. ft of real estate globally and cost the group $1 billion (around ₹ 4680 crores now) of its annual combined revenue of $13.6 billion. 'In a business where our second biggest investment is property, it's important,' qualifies Sorrell, as he describes a range of creative spaces, from 'Grey's wonderful new building in Union Square' to another WPP agency that operates from a converted railway yard in Zurich.

Equally, he proclaims that 'when you walk into the front door (of WPP), the last thing you should think is that this is the headquarters of the largest advertising and marketing services company in the world.' He clarifies the dichotomy by pointing out that the role of the parent company is a staff function, not an operational, revenue-producing role, and must therefore remain lean, eschewing lavish excesses.

WPP's offices have been strictly carved out of the existing spaces occupied by other WPP group agencies–reflecting Sorrell's pragmatism–rather than any desire to build an iconic building for the global headquarters.

The location for Sorrell's London office, 27 Farm Street, is a set of two converted, pre-1930s' town houses, on a quiet road off Berkeley Square, Mayfair's prestigious centrepiece. It is spectacularly unassuming. The bright yellow front door attracts passers-by, but the actual entrance is tucked under an archway, around the corner,

The WPP office is housed in a set of two converted, pre-1930s town houses in London's Mayfair neighbourhood

which has better access to the space. If anything, the building itself is a metaphor for Sorrell's approach to his business. This hybrid of two town houses merged into one operating space is analogous to the multi-bodied WPP, a conglomerate of more than 150 agencies, stacked together by acquisition over the years.

'When you walk into the front door (of WPP), the last thing you should think is that this is the headquarters of the largest advertising and marketing services company in the world.'

The office's earlier occupant was the regional head of European operations of J. Walter Thompson (JWT), the first major WPP acquisition in 1987. After the takeover, Sorrell concluded that it made more sense for JWT's regional head to be based at the agency's main offices in Berkeley Square, a few minutes away, and that the Farm Street offices were better utilized for WPP's corporate headquarters. In New York, where Sorrell spends half his time, WPP's office footprint has similarly kept pace with its acquisitions. His first New York office was in the same building as JWT, followed, for many years, by one in the same buildings as Ogilvy and Mather, a rival agency that WPP acquired in 1989. WPP in New York now occupies space in the offices that earlier belonged to TNS, a market research firm and recent acquisition.

It is this fiscal discipline that has allowed him to successfully create and operate a monolithic

'There is a correlation between office plan and energy.'

empire in an industry earlier dominated by individual fiefdoms and small hot-shops. This pragmatism is underlined by Sorrell's no-nonsense attitude towards the advertising and marketing services industry, which he says 'failed to acknowledge, that it was a business', prior to his consolidation spree.

Sustainable creativity

Our conversation on workplaces also captures another pronounced Sorrell trait–the ability to grasp big-picture ideas (such as the role of the parent company versus the role of the individual agency), and to translate them into practical detail (tangible bricks-and-mortar offices).

Just as Sorrell maintains financial conservatism for the parent company, he recognizes that an inspiring workplace can stimulate the creativity that is the lifeline of WPP agencies, remarking that 'there is a correlation between office plan and energy'.

Sorrell is well aware of the physical dimensions of individual agencies, and unlike most chief executives, has made it his business to correlate workplace design with business issues. 'The biggest problem in our business is getting people to work together,' he analyses. The open-plan Buenos Aires office found its way into the WPP's annual report because he realized that tearing down walls was a valuable architectural device to foster collaboration, which would move companies towards a 'networked organization structure', rather than traditional, 'siloed' divisional units.

The bright yellow front door looks welcoming, but the actual entrance is tucked under an archway, around the corner

Since then, WPP has devised a Space Programme–an online platform where agencies within the network can confidentially share best practices in managing real estate, through creative, cost-effective use of space. In keeping with the climate change zeitgeist, Sorrell also lists energy-efficient buildings as a focus area in reducing waste, citing the ubiquitous phrase of 'green business is good business'.

'The biggest problem in our business is getting people to work together.'

Growth plans

Our conversation on workplace is timely. WPP celebrated its twenty-fifth anniversary in May and Sorrell's journey towards global domination began with 'two people in a room the size of this conference room', as he has often said earlier. Twenty-five years and 1,38,000 employees later, his personal office, on the floor above us, is probably about the same size as the conference room.

This apparent contradiction parallels Sorrell's curious role within WPP. He is the founder of the global conglomerate, its chief executive, the face of the parent brand, and yet only a minority (albeit wealthy) shareholder, with less than 2 per cent ownership of the company. His position is especially unusual for observers accustomed to India's promoter-driven business environment, where company management, ownership and public relations are usually embodied in a single individual. For Sorrell, corporate ambition is clearly not defined merely by the amount of individual shareholding, or the size of the chief executive's office.

6 September 2010

RAJAN ANANDAN

Rajan Anandan of Google works off a height-adjustable desk

THE ENERGETIC IDEATOR

Even in India, the headquarters of the global company most synonymous with 'cool' workplaces is Google, which occupies seven floors of a commercial building in Gurgaon, Haryana. I am waiting to meet Rajan Anandan, managing director and vice president, sales and operations, of Google South East Asia and India. Anandan joined the Internet services firm as a senior-level lateral hire in 2011, after having held leadership roles in technology companies Dell and Microsoft in India.

Like many of his peers in the Internet industry, he works off a desk in an open office on the first floor, rather than from a private cabin of his own, with one difference: all the desks are height-adjustable, enabling occupants to stand and work. It is an ergonomic (albeit expensive) feature to support better posture at work, and I noticed several employees standing and working.

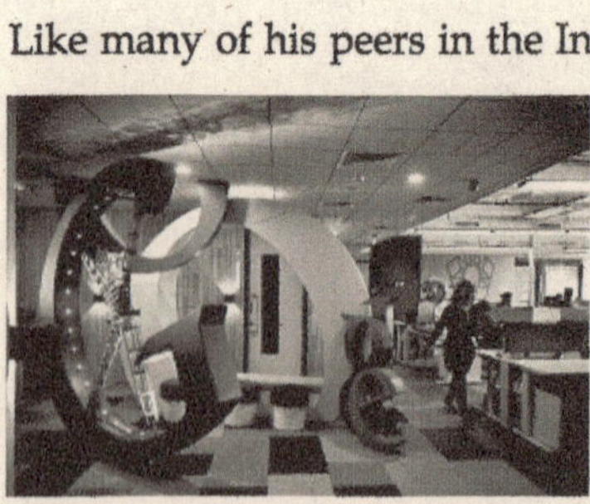

Breakout areas are scattered across the floor

'Meetings are the death of speed.'

Despite a growing body of research that suggests that open-plan offices are unproductive and inefficient, Anandan says: 'I wouldn't trade this for a million because of the pulse of the place. I can see all my leaders; I can see all my younger colleagues, the person next to me is twenty-four years old. If I want the pulse of the place, I just ask how it's going.'

When he needs privacy, for meetings or calls, Anandan moves to a small meeting room that is largely dedicated for his use, although others can reserve it too. 'Having an open office without private spaces is a bad idea. When you have meetings, it becomes very noisy,' he says.

Multiple work settings are extremely important for efficiency, says Anandan, and that's why Google has different kinds of meeting spaces–'phone booths' for people to make a call or work, compact meeting rooms for small meetings, larger rooms for bigger team meetings and 'a really large room where I have my leadership team meeting every Monday'.

The rest of the office conforms to the Silicon Valley stereotype of a 'funky' or 'wacky' workspace, where the boundaries between work and play are blurred. At the reception, visitors can choose to wait inside a pair of old-fashioned train compartments. An installation of a flock of sheep welcomes visitors. Micro-kitchens on every floor help stave off hunger pangs. The breakout areas are striking, inviting and scattered across each floor. Employees can play table tennis, pool, foosball, air hockey and other games in the recreation area, or go to one of the several sleep pods for a quick nap. This is all bound together by a graphic scheme which is vibrant, lively and cohesive, without being excessive.

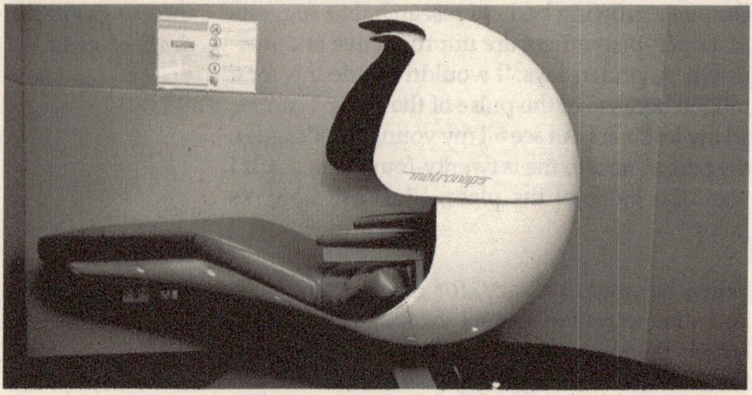

A sleep pod for quick naps

Strategy at work

It is tempting to be sceptical about Google's workplace, which can seem indulgent or wasteful at first glance, but my conversation with Anandan helps me understand exactly why Google's trademark offices are part of the company's business strategy, and how they reinforce specific work styles.

'Think 10x, not 10 per cent.'

In their book *How Google Works* (2014), authors Eric Schmidt and Jonathan Rosenberg describe these work styles as examples of a 'smart creative', or someone who is 'business-savvy, has technical knowledge, creative energy and a hands-on approach to getting things done'–qualities Anandan seems to embody.

First, agility. Being able to stand and work, and being able to 'stay on the pulse', helps Anandan to stay agile, which is both a personality trait and an element of company culture–he speaks quickly, is energetic, and rarely stays in one place for long. 'Meetings are the death of speed' is a common Anandan refrain.

Second, empowerment. The workplace is a direct expression of the company's belief that in order to achieve extraordinary results, Google employees must be provided with an extraordinary environment. 'Think 10x, not 10 per cent' is another Anandan mantra. 'We have very rigorous hiring processes, we hire the smartest, most passionate people in the world, and everyone has very ambitious goals, moon shot thinking. Every team is trying to come up with plans that are truly breakthrough,' says Anandan.

'The only thing that will continue to make us relevant ten years from now will be our ability to innovate, our ability to be agile, our ability to hire the best people, our ability to continue to connect in this crazy environment.'

Rigorous hiring and empowered goal-setting exercises are accompanied by an equally rigorous performance evaluation system. 'We are very clear on deliverables and we measure outcomes rigorously,' explains Anandan, adding that the company operates on ninety-day planning cycles and six-monthly performance reviews of both quantitative and qualitative goals.

Providing employees with the right resources to achieve their targets is also vital. 'It's no point saying "go climb Mount Everest, but I am not going to give you an oxygen tank," you probably will die on the way,' says Anandan. An inspiring and creative work environment, which promotes individual empowerment and raises performance expectations, is an important resource.

Innovation culture

Third, out-of-the-box thinking, which is second nature to innovative companies such as Google (Anandan mentions the word 'idea' fifteen times in our conversation, more than most). 'The only thing that will continue to make us relevant ten years from now will be our ability to innovate, our ability to be agile, our ability to hire the best people, our ability to continue to connect in this crazy environment, always on top of things. And that's what the game is,' he says.

The graphic design scheme is lively and vibrant

Keeping updated is the first step. 'I read tech blogs, I read everything online, and because personally I do a lot of angel investing, I am totally on top of the trends,' he says. This helps him develop acumen. 'In our space, there is a lot of stuff that is not real yet. Everything becomes real at some point. So the judgement call is when does it become real?'

Finally, vigilance. Google operates within an important paradox: Although it has an open, accessible, user-led philosophy, it must take security and privacy seriously. For example, I find the accepted practice among individuals in positions of leadership and power, of relying on a free Gmail service for their personal email, quite ironic–it just doesn't seem secure enough. Anandan disagrees, pointing out that 'the world-scale infrastructure we run is the most secure in the world', and 'we have rigorous processes around data privacy, around use of privacy and data security'.

The workplace captures this dichotomy. For all its openness, the company has among the tightest security checks at its entrance that I've experienced, with an X-ray machine in addition to mandatory security clearances. As any 'smart creative' would know, any company wanting to remain digitally omniscient must know how to draw boundaries in the real world too.

For all its openness, the company has among the tightest security checks at its entrance that I've experienced, with an X-ray machine in addition to mandatory security clearances.

19 April 2015

PURPOSE

Management literature emphasizes the role of purpose as central to authentic and effective leadership. Warren Bennis, a global authority on leadership, underlines this point in an essay titled *'Leading Managers to Adapt and Grow'* in *Business: The Ultimate Resource* (2002), a compendium on best practice in business. 'The capacity to engage followers in shared meaning–to align the stars around a common, meaningful goal, not just any old goal, (but) "a mission from God", is one of four critical ingredients of leaderships, he says, going on to state that the others include resilience, emotional intelligence and having a moral compass.

The design of a workplace makes it easy to understand the occupant's purpose. Physical assets often reveal a leader's real priorities, and help to identify if, and how, a chief executive is aligning the organization around its stated purpose.

For example, the new Tata Hall and the innovation lab at the Harvard Business School campus are architectural evidence of the school's dean, Nitin Nohria's stated intent 'to innovate in educational programmes' and 'to internationalize to increase the school's global reach and impact'.

Equally, Kotak's new corporate headquarters expresses founder Uday Kotak's desire to construct a 'practical, efficient facility', with extensive collaboration spaces for clients and employees.

NITIN NOHRIA

Nohria likes meeting visitors at his four-seater discussion table

THE COSMOPOLITAN OPTIMIST

A wall-mounted sculpture of the Hindu god Ganesha hangs above a surrealistic print of green cats and floating goldfish–an eclectic combination of artwork in a corporate office, but something of a personal talisman for Nitin Nohria, the dean of Harvard Business School (HBS).

Nohria says this particular arrangement has accompanied him to every office since he first began teaching at the business school in the US in 1988. Ganesha, of course, augurs good beginnings, while the print is the first piece of art Nohria bought–for $1 (₹ 56), at a roadside garage sale. 'It caught my eye when I was driving. What I love about it is that it evokes curiosity,' he says.

A photograph of Nohria with three of his predecessors

The artwork–like the rest of the items in Nohria's sunlit office in Morgan Hall on the HBS campus in Boston–shines a light on one of his most defining traits: cosmopolitan leadership. Nohria's collection of paintings, posters, rugs and artefacts straddle several continents and decades and reflect long-standing professional and personal interests and friendships. Books on business management and economic theory are placed alongside decorative African and Chinese artefacts. Modern Indian art and family photographs rub shoulders with a framed photograph of the Boston Celtics basketball team in action, given to Nohria by Paul Polman, multinational firm Unilever's chief executive officer.

'We want people to genuinely have global vision but also remain rooted in local understandings, and we're trying to find that combination–always.'

Cosmopolitan leadership is a trait Nohria personifies, having grown up in India and worked in the US. It is also one which he espouses at the school. 'We want people to genuinely have global vision but also remain rooted in local understandings, and we're trying to find that combination–always,' he says. For Nohria, the business school is 'an American institution operating in a global century, rooted in its place, where the interests of America are deeply important to us', yet which is 'more global than any other business school in terms of the intellectual reach of our school'. Certainly the HBS 'brand', manifest in its trademark case studies, monthly journal, faculty and alumni, has an extremely well-travelled footprint.

Managing paradoxes

Being internationally minded, however, is only one aspect of Nohria's version of 'cosmopolitan leadership'. The trickier paradox is to remain both humble and ambitious; to respect and learn from others, yet retain enough self-confidence to drive change. This outlook is particularly vital for someone in Nohria's position as head of a 100-year-old institution with more than 200 independently minded faculty, and a brand synonymous with management education. HBS is also a hefty organization, with 1100 full-time staff positions, $500 million (₹ 3100 crores) in revenue for the

The presidential-style desk in Nohria's office

fiscal year ended 30 June 2011, and a $2.8 billion (₹ 17,421.6 crores) endowment.

Nohria's changes in the dean's office, since he took charge two years ago suggest that he is selectively retaining and renewing various elements. He replaced the room's wall-to-wall carpet with rugs, but retained the furniture. The room is large enough to accommodate a presidential desk, a four-seater discussion table and a few cabinets and bookshelves. He meets people at a four-seater discussion table ('it's intimate and to human scale') in his office rather than at the presidential-style desk.

He meets people at a four-seater discussion table ('it's intimate and to human scale') in his office rather than at the presidential-style desk.

A photograph of Nohria on the bookshelf with three predecessors–John McArthur, Kim Clark and Jay Light–is, he says, 'a very important picture for me. This represents thirty years of deans at HBS, almost a third of the history of the school.' Next to it is an architectural model of the proposed Tata Hall for executive education, which is under construction. Nohria acknowledges that the campus' impressive architecture is part of its 'enduring legacy' and that he feels responsible for its 'continuing evolution'.

Morality and power

'I love dark movies, the capacity for people in power to do good and bad things has always fascinated me.'

There cannot be a more pressing time to take stock of the school's legacy, both physical and intellectual. The financial crisis of 2008 provoked serious questions on ethics in management education. Some prominent HBS alumni–most notably, former Enron president Jeff Skilling, and more recently, former Goldman Sachs director Rajat Gupta–have ironically fulfilled the school's promise 'to educate leaders who make a difference in the world' in an unintended manner, with negative results.

Two very different items in Nohria's office highlight his preoccupation with power and morality: an early edition of Adam Smith's *The Wealth of Nations*, a treasured gift from a friend, and a poster of the film, *The Godfather*, starring Marlon Brando given to him by former students. 'I love dark movies, the capacity for people in power to do good and bad things has always fascinated me,' he says.

Nohria is passionately optimistic about business as a force for good. 'The greatest invention in the world, to my mind, is the business enterprise, because it is a sustainable venture which relies on self-interest,' he argues, explaining that 'being self-interested is not the same as self-centred. Adam Smith actually says that what distinguishes businesspeople are their moral sentiments, of still recognizing that as they pursue what they do, they can do it in a way that is in the interest of society.'

Nohria's earliest works of art include a Ganesha sculpture and a quirky print

He hopes to enable students to imbibe these learnings through radical additions to the MBA curriculum, such as practical, field-based learning, where students travel to emerging countries and work in teams alongside existing companies to devise new products and services. New cases

'The greatest invention in the world, to my mind, is the business enterprise, because it is a sustainable venture which relies on self-interest. Being self-interested is not the same as self-centred.'

have also been written about leaders who lost direction when in power. An 'innovation lab' on campus was opened six months ago to facilitate more real-life, group-based work.

'I believe that we will have students experience much more, in a vibrant way, what it means to be in power, and then have some memory of that, what it means to be powerful,' he says, explaining, 'If there are powerful memories, then they can be triggered, and can change behaviour in interesting ways.'

Nohria's optimism is not without its challenges. The abundant HBS campus, built over the course of a century, with tennis courts, lounges and a country club atmosphere, is more easily associated with living the good life than anything else. He admits that it can be construed as a 'bubble, separated from the rest of the world', but is committed to his personal endeavour. 'I deeply believe that we need to remind people that this is the most honourable thing that you can do. I will only feel good if people will say the mission statement at HBS is not just an empty bunch of words,' he reiterates. A hope for both a more prosperous society, and its business leaders, perhaps.

1 July 2012

With no fancy furniture or lighting, this banker's office reflects a mix of 'hard' functionality and 'soft' culture

UDAY KOTAK

THE PURPOSEFUL ENTREPRENEUR

I don't expect many surprises during my visit to the second floor of the Bakhtawar building at Mumbai's Nariman Point. This is the office of Uday Kotak, executive vice chairman and managing director of Kotak Mahindra Bank Ltd. At first glance, it meets my slender expectations of the archetypal banker's workplace. But a closer look helps in understanding how Kotak managed to create one of India's most successful conglomerates.

Functional space

The corporate headquarters and CEO workspaces of Indian financial institutions–or the ones I've visited so far, at least–tend to emphasize function over form, prioritizing efficiency over aesthetic flourishes. Kotak's office is no different; a mid-sized cabin with a slightly outdated interior palette, bland furniture, nice terrace garden, potted plants, some artwork and extremely limited paraphernalia. What makes the cabin seem boxed is the floor's layout. Like in many Nariman Point buildings, Kotak

A personalized portrait given to each Kotak employee when the bank gained its banking licence in 2003

'Most of the challenges the financial services industry faces today come from the clash between the two models–the saver- borrower model, and the issuer-investor model. And my view is that the dynamics of some of these businesses are pretty dramatically different.'

Mahindra's office too seems cramped and awkward, with small rooms and narrow corridors, when compared with today's open-plan floor plates and expansive suites.

The cabin has remained largely unchanged since he first occupied it in the late 1990s, Kotak says. Relocation to a new office block, in the more contemporary Bandra Kurla Complex neighbourhood, is scheduled for early next year. The new facility will physically integrate several business units, now scattered across the city. But he clarifies with trademark pragmatism: 'We don't want to make it a "dream office". We just want to make it a good, solid, efficient, functional office.'

The objects in the office also capture several important nuances in Kotak's approach to the banking industry–in fact, the particular selection of items on display is as notable as the absence of other frills.

Clarity and focus

A framed copy of Rudyard Kipling's poem *If*, given by a friend, sits on a shelf next to one of the room's large windows. 'It's good,' he remarks. The piece exudes stoicism, advocating perseverance with one's mission and sense of purpose, beginning with the famous lines *'If you can keep your head when all about you/Are losing theirs and blaming it on you…'*

A framed copy of Rudyard Kipling's poem *If*, given by a friend

The poem resonates with my impressions of his character. A senior Kotak Mahindra client who knows Kotak well describes him as someone with immense ability to focus during a particular discussion, even though he may be grappling with other issues elsewhere. He is also respected for his ability to present a balanced viewpoint to clients, conveying both confidence and caution, as appropriate to the situation.

For Kotak, clarity about one's business model is vital to success. 'Most of the challenges the financial services industry faces today come from the clash between the two models–the saver-borrower model, and the issuer-investor model. And my view is that the dynamics of some of these businesses are pretty dramatically different,' he says.

'The bank of the future must have three human qualities. Prudence, simplicity in services and products, and humility.'

Many banks, including Kotak Mahindra, operate in both spheres, through traditional lending channels as well as through capital market and asset management units, which are driven by the latter model. But risks to business viability can be mitigated by 'building sustainable trust' and adhering to values, says Kotak.

Next to the poem are a number of awards won by the bank, all recognizing it for being an employer of choice. Of the several awards the bank has won during its twenty-six-year history, it's interesting to note that Kotak has chosen to keep human resource-related accolades on his desk.

Behind Kotak's desk is a selection of group photographs with colleagues, some taken nearly a decade ago, others more recent. One of the more weathered images is a mock cover of the *Business India* magazine with Kotak on the front, titled '*Creating History*'. Each employee was given a similar personalized portrait in 2003 when the company gained a banking licence, Kotak recounts, clarifying that 'I was given one in my capacity as an employee. It was an important year for us.' The company employed 1500 people at the time; today there are 22,000.

Staying grounded

Kotak's grounded approach to his workplace can be seen as a metaphor for his resolve to remain balanced in business. 'The bank of the future

'Bankers genuinely believe they are masters of the universe, when they are actually in the business of serving customers.'

must have three human qualities,' says Kotak. First, prudence, in terms of avoiding too much leverage that would put the entire organization at risk. 'I am by nature a believer that you grow the store, but be very careful before you bet the store.' Second, simplicity in services and products, so that customers fully understand any transaction's fine print.

Third, and most importantly for Kotak, is humility. 'Bankers genuinely believe they are masters of the universe, when they are actually in the business of serving customers,' he points out, emphasizing that 'one of the most important challenges for a financial sector player or a bank is building trust with customers'.

This is a responsibility that professionals often 'take very lightly', which is ironic, given that financial institutions themselves are highly leveraged. It is a sensible prescription of virtues, and combined with Kotak's astute entrepreneurial instinct, helps in understanding how he steadily expanded his modest bill discounting firm in 1986, into a multi-pronged financial conglomerate, currently valued at ₹ 43,800 crores, when many aspirants have fallen by the wayside.

Building an institution

Kotak's long-standing desire has been to 'build a high-quality, trustworthy financial institution', in the same vein as banks such as Goldman Sachs and J.P. Morgan, which were named after individuals, but grew beyond their original founders and their families. It is an ambitious goal–unlike Kotak Mahindra, most respected large-scale Indian financial institutions have had some public sector backing.

Mementoes in Kotak's office

His sense of the critical ingredients in creating such an organization is somewhat unexpected–not 'hard numbers, but soft stuff like culture. My obsession is to build a culture which makes people trust us,' he states. The statement indicates his preoccupation with his long-term mission, alongside meeting short-term financial goals. Most chief executives tend to have a less acute sense of the importance of corporate culture in building competitive advantage.

'One of the most important challenges for a financial sector player or a bank is building trust with customers. My obsession is to build a culture which makes people trust us.'

Right now, improving internal communication between different business verticals is a key objective in creating a collaborative, homogenous, firm-wide culture, he explains. To attain as much credibility as its more established peers, the bank will also need a cadre of professionals, who are regarded as senior industry leaders in their own right.

He acknowledges the challenges with characteristic candour. 'I think we have made some progress, but I frankly feel we have a long way to go, to create and build a brand which has the ability to withstand hundreds of years.' The proposed new office building appears to signify an inflection point, in more ways than one, for both the individual and the institution.

5 September 2012

UPDATE: *Kotak Mahindra moved into a new corporate headquarters in Bandra Kurla Complex in August 2013.*

SECTION III: BRAND VALUES

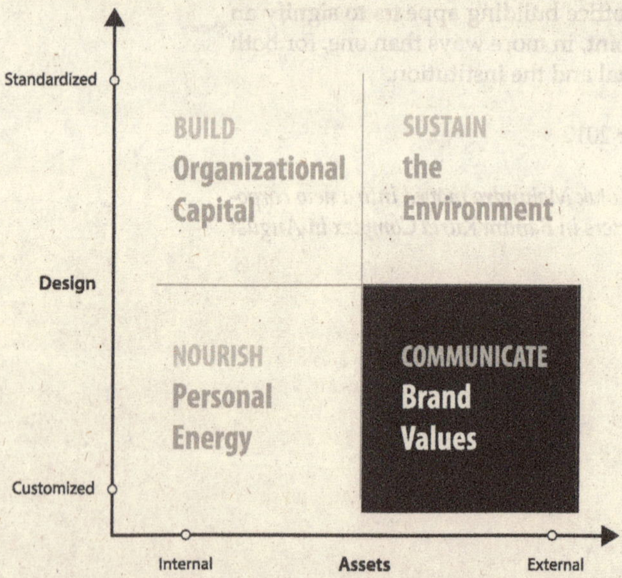

PLATFORM TO COMMUNICATE BRAND VALUES

A chief executive with a slide outside his cabin; an office with writable walls and beanbags; or one with images of fashion legends in every conference room–these are archetypal workplaces designed for 'liberalization's children'; 'cool' offices for a youthful, digital and vocal workforce.

Those who might be tempted to dismiss these offices as frivolous or indulgent would do well to look closer at the subtext of the work environment, and specifically at the brand messages being communicated.

Brands are potent intangible assets; a brand's reputation can determine whether a company thrives, or just survives. Although branding is primarily associated with marketing and communication, progressive business leaders are now gravitating to the idea of 'narrative workplaces' and to the notion that employees should experience the brand in an immersive, three-dimensional way at work.

Workplace experts Jeremy Myerson and Philip Ross highlight this global trend in office design in their book, *The 21st Century Office* (2003). 'What is so striking about the new cluster of narrative office projects is the commitment to making the office environment a substantial tool in the business of brand differentiation.... inside a narrative office, you "live and breathe" the brand... This approach reflects the view that marketing is no longer a discrete function–all office staff are perceived to be in the marketing front-line, and the spaces in which they work have become prime platforms to communicate brand ethos all day long.'

Such workplaces share a common outlook, regardless of industry. 'What characterizes all narrative offices is a sense of playfulness and surprise,' Myerson and Ross observe, before concluding 'the narrative trend is a way to banish the bland office interior'.

Brand values can be showcased in different ways–to encourage **innovative thinking**, to express one's **personality** or to use spaces to **tell stories** around the brand's ideology.

DESIGN TRIGGERS FOR A 'NARRATIVE' WORKPLACE:

1. *Which brand values would you like your employees to imbibe?*
2. *How would you like to express your organization's identity in the workplace?*
3. *Can you bring your brand to life through stories or metaphors?*
4. *Which design elements would you like to use to depict your brand? For example: vertical surfaces, conference room names, architectural elements such as columns, public spaces such as the reception or more?*
5. *Which colours, materials and finishes will best express your brand?*
6. *Which graphic tools would you like to use: images, typography, icons or more?*
7. *Would you like to create 'brand experiences' for co-workers in the workplace?*
8. *Which branded elements would you like to be dynamic and which can be static?*
9. *Will you reinforce your brand through digital and technological touchpoints?*
10. *Can you provide dedicated spaces for collaborative project work?*

INNOVATION

'To be creative, a place does not have to be crazy, kooky and located in northern California. What is a prerequisite is an environment–social but also spatial–in which people know they can experiment, take risks and explore the full range of their faculties.

It does little good to identify the brightest T-shaped people around, assemble them in interdisciplinary teams, and network them to other teams if they are forced to work in an environment that dooms their efforts from the start. The physical and psychological spaces of an organization work in tandem to define the effectiveness of the people within it,' states Tim Brown, the president and chief executive officer of Ideo, one of the world's best known design firms, in his book *Change by Design* (2009).

In other words, the best designed workplaces should ignite innovative thinking. To my mind, there are few better examples than the office of Park Won-Soon, the mayor of Seoul, whose quirky office magnifies his commitment to social innovation. It was inspiring to see an elected government official with so much faith in creativity and the power of intangibles.

The office of Kiran Mazumdar-Shaw, chairman and founder of biotech company Biocon, captures a different aspect of innovation: risk-taking and experimentation.

KIRAN MAZUMDAR-SHAW

The Biocon head designed the office with comfort as a key criteria

THE ADAPTABLE INNOVATOR

A wood-panelled office in the executive suite of a twenty-acre campus in Bangalore's Electronics City is a reviewer's delight. This is the personal workspace of Kiran Mazumdar-Shaw, chairman and managing director of biopharma company Biocon Ltd. Unlike others, her office is packed with memorabilia, which showcase her several avatars.

First, Mazumdar-Shaw as business achiever; there are photographs of her with political leaders and dignitaries such as US President Barack Obama, Prime Minister Manmohan Singh and former President A.P.J. Abdul Kalam. Second, as industry pioneer; there are framed certificates of her honorary doctorate degrees in science, for recognizing her contribution to biotechnology, from the University of Glasgow in Scotland, Trinity College Dublin in Ireland, and from her alma mater, University of Ballarat, Australia, where she first qualified as a master brewer.

Her office serves as a gallery for her art collection

Third, as chief executive officer; alongside the usual office mementoes, a red, fabric-bound book rests on a shelf behind Mazumdar-Shaw's desk. It is a compilation of photographs and press stories chronicling her journey over several decades, put together by colleagues for her fifty-ninth birthday; a simple, yet affectionate gesture.

'Because I spend so much time here, I feel I should enjoy my workplace, and I tend to make it as homely as possible.'

Long-standing personal relationships are clearly important to Mazumdar-Shaw; she has kept letters and greeting cards from legendary scientist and Nobel Prize winner James Watson, whom she says she 'knows very well'. Family photographs, including those of her late father, are prominently placed, both behind the desk and under the glass on the desk. She has also preserved a childhood drawing from her nephew, who wrote, 'If I found a pot of gold I would give it to my aunt for her company to make new medicines for very bad diseases.'

Finally, and most visibly, the office serves as a gallery for Mazumdar-Shaw the art collector, with paintings and sculptures by Scottish artists and Indian masters, such as Yusuf Arakkal and M.F. Husain. The lively artwork animates her chamber, the waiting room outside, the boardroom next door and the surroundings of the verdant campus itself. Both Mazumdar-Shaw and her husband, John Shaw, vice chairman of Biocon, whose office is right next to hers, are self-professed 'avid art lovers'.

Mazumdar-Shaw says she designed the office herself, with comfort as the key criteria. 'Because I spend so much time here, I feel I should enjoy my workplace, and I tend to make it as homely as possible.' The widespread presence of personal artefacts certainly lends warmth and a 'living-room' feel to the space.

A red fabric-bound book with a compilation of photographs and press stories rests on a shelf behind Mazumar-Shaw's desk

Forward-thinking builder

While the stack of awards and citations illustrate Mazumdar-Shaw's business standing, I believe the space also casts a light on a less obvious, and perhaps more compelling, aspect of her personality: her ability to innovate. Despite its old-world aesthetic, the office captures two nuances of her approach towards the business of innovation.

'More than being a risk-taker, I manage risk very well, I take calculated risks, I don't make wild bets.'

These help in understanding how she progressed from being a garage entrepreneur in 1978, making industrial enzymes, to the head of a leading biopharmaceutical corporation which now serves global customers and has subsidiaries in research and clinical development.

First, on managing the inherent tension between risk and opportunity, associated with any sort of innovation. How can one ensure that experimental investments pay off, without jeopardizing the company? Mazumdar-Shaw professes that 'more than being a risk-taker, I manage risk very well, I take calculated risks, I don't make wild bets' but equally, 'I think ahead, I'm futuristic, I have a lot of hope and confidence.'

Biocon's business model, as she has often stated,

is 'risk-balanced with a portfolio of bio-similars, generics and novel programmes', she says. Profits from 'more predictable and assured programmes' are invested in research-led innovation, such as the oral insulin programme which the company has been working on for the last six years. 'If it works, it will be transformational for the company, but I have not bet the company on it,' she elaborates.

'I needed space. I said I will not be in my garage for the rest of my life. I knew I needed manufacturing, I didn't want twenty acres, but this came as a distress sale.'

This calibrated approach to risk and opportunity is evident in Mazumdar-Shaw's decision to invest in a twenty-acre campus as early as 1983. I was surprised to learn how quickly Mazumdar-Shaw scaled her office space–starting out in a garage in 1978, she moved into a rented, two bedroom home in 1980, after which she directly expanded to a twenty-acre campus in 1983. 'I needed space. I said I will not be in my garage for the rest of my life. I knew I needed manufacturing, I didn't want twenty acres, but this came as a distress sale,' she recalls.

It is a classic example of an optimistic, yet measured, investment. Since then, the company has expanded manufacturing operations, which now include a larger, ninety-acre campus in Bangalore.

Second, Mazumdar-Shaw clearly believes in building on existing strengths to maximize new opportunities. Biocon's first 'game-changing moment' took place when she decided to trade up from manufacturing industrial enzymes to making and marketing patented enzymes for the first time in the mid-1980s, she says. The strategy of employing existing product knowledge and investing in new technologies worked, and the company attracted global customers.

Photographs of Kiran Mazumdar-Shaw with various dignitaries

The next transformational moment entailed 'leveraging all that we've learnt in enzymes and

'By leveraging all that we've learnt in enzymes and applying it to pharmaceuticals, we were able to enter the pharmaceutical market in a differentiated way.'

applying it to pharmaceuticals', she describes, by which she was 'able to enter the pharmaceutical market in a differentiated way'. Subsequent market success allowed her to both broaden and deepen the company's research capabilities and pursue more ambitious projects.

Adaptability appears to be at the heart of this innovation model, which entails building on one's strengths, while constantly looking for opportunities to transform oneself and add new competencies–in effect, being simultaneously rooted and restless.

Her office serves as a spatial metaphor for this model; Mazumdar-Shaw still uses the same desk as in her garage days ('I'm sentimental'). Equally, the varied art in her room underlines her ability to look outward and develop an appreciation for new ideas.

Innovation is currently a much-contested subject in corporate India. Mazumdar-Shaw has publicly argued that Biocon is 'undervalued', and that the company's innovation capabilities are not fully appreciated. Biocon's consolidated revenue has nearly quadrupled since its initial public offering in 2004, but its market capitalization has not yet doubled in the same period: there are still many critics to convince.

In its own way, Mazumdar-Shaw's physical space captures her outlook towards business innovation: balance risk, extract opportunities and harness one's strengths, at all times.

9 December 2012

Park at his desk stacked with piles of paper several feet high

PARK WON-SOON

THE SOCIAL INNOVATOR

I visited a most peculiar–and the most interesting–office so far in this series. It contained a kitchen garden, furniture made from recycled wood, disjointed bookshelves, a patchwork wall of Post-it notes and various columns of paper stacked several feet high. Its inhabitant is not an eccentric academic, as one might assume, but someone holding a powerful political position in his country.

Meet Park Won-Soon, the mayor of Seoul, a grass-roots anti-corruption activist and former human rights lawyer, who contested and won the mayoral election as an independent candidate in October 2011.

The unusual workspace captures Park's distinct political ideology, his personal charisma and idiosyncrasies–some of which underline my reasons for visiting South Korea. I was in Seoul to speak at a conference on social innovation and cities, co-hosted by the Seoul Metropolitan Government and the Social Innovation Exchange, a global non-profit network of thinkers and doers in the social sphere.

A cartoon showing Park growing older

'I want to start with small but definitive change; the big picture is too abstract.'

Creative political symbolism

Each item in Park's office has a story. The handwritten Post-it notes at the entrance are specific requests and suggestions by citizens urging him to 'build more playgrounds' or 'create more jobs', for example.

Park received them during his election campaign and inauguration; they are consistent with Park's campaign slogan that 'Citizens are the mayor'. They also serve as a daily reminder of the need to focus on 'the small and the trivial things in citizens' everyday lives', he says, rather than big-budget projects which add to the city's deficit and do not improve everyday life for all. He adds: 'I want to start with small but definitive change; the big picture is too abstract.' Better pavement construction; eco-friendly, free school lunches; and more public rental housing are personal milestones for Park.

In the corner of his office, herbs and vegetables grow in a kitchen garden to highlight how farming can flourish in compact urban spaces such as apartments, workspaces and rooftops. Park would like to see residents forming local farming cooperatives and sharing their harvest, as a sign of more sharing in general between Seoul citizens.

The creative symbolism extends to his office furniture. A wedge of bookshelves is artfully inserted between two deliberately slanted cabinets to join them. The slanted shelves represent social gaps 'between rich and poor, the left and the right, elderly and young. My vision is to be a bridge,' explains Park. Elsewhere, a meeting table is made of recycled wood by a carpenter from a social enterprise, who refashioned material from old wardrobes, shoe shelves and drawers into a table.

A piece of furniture made from recycled wood

A wedge of bookshelves artfully inserted between two deliberately slanted cabinets to join them

Park's desk is surrounded by stacks of paper, on a par with the most bureaucratic government office one might find anywhere in the world. 'I don't have time to sit in this chair, so the papers are growing like trees,' he laughs. 'But I can find all the papers I need,' Park adds.

Personalized artwork proliferates on every available surface–a cartoon showing Park growing older, a children's drawing of Seoul, a small poster with 'Big Ear leadership', highlighting his desire to be perceived as a leader who listens to his constituents, and a cardboard placard with 'Social Designer' on it–an unusual epithet.

The slanted shelves represent social gaps 'between rich and poor, the left and the right, elderly and young. My vision is to be a bridge.'

Park likes to think of himself as a 'social innovator'–or someone who uses creativity, empathy and insight to generate user-driven, innovative solutions to tricky social challenges. 'The answer is always at the site of the problem,' he says, adding that he spends many hours travelling on local trains or visiting public housing projects to understand the citizens' challenges himself, in the same way as professional designers dig deep to understand user needs when trying to come up with new products or services.

Finally, there is a documentary-style short video

'The answer is always at the site of the problem.'

of Park's office, running in the visitor waiting space outside his suite, where he explains the design logic of the space, in Korean and English.

I've been to several creative workspaces over the years, but never have I met someone who has so deliberately–and cost-effectively–leveraged his office as a personalized communication tool with his target audience. Park's offbeat workspace might warrant scepticism about his governance approach. The symbolism in his office might even seem gimmicky or self-promotional.

But, he's on to something: the citizen-oriented ideology has made him popular with constituents. Even the few businesspeople I spoke to in Seoul, who point out that he's not as focused on business as his predecessors, concede that he is doing good work for the city.

Citizens, communities and institutions

Park explains the rationale behind his ideology by outlining his assessment of Seoul's challenges. Rapid economic development in Korea over several decades resulted in dwindling individual interest in public affairs, as well as increased corruption, he says. His prescription: citizen-led, environmentally friendly, community-oriented governance, which will strengthen society and thus result in a more robust economy.

Lessons from Seoul

So what insight does this rather quirky mayor in a highly developed city, several thousand kilometres away, have to offer us?

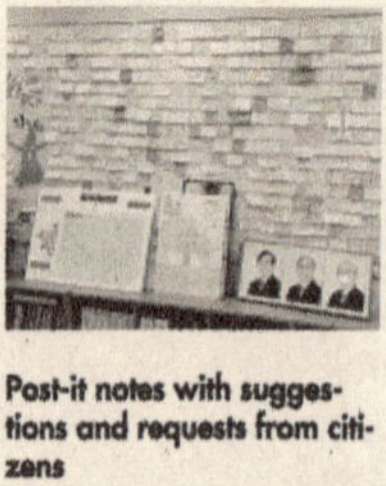

Post-it notes with suggestions and requests from citizens

First, Park's approach to democracy can be replicated in other countries, by other players. In fact, US President Barack Obama's path to power is similar–grass-roots activism, community mobilization and public life experience as a lawyer.

Park's success seems to lie in his ability to build and scale institutions (such as a second-hand goods retailer, and a think-and-do tank) thus mobilizing people and resources in effective ways. Along the way, he has been quick to adopt new ideas and tools such as social innovation or social media, which help him to remain connected, and relevant, to a younger audience.

'I'm always trying to invite citizens to participate in the process of public decision-making. That's the reason why I'm trying to establish various institutions.'

Second, his governance approach highlights that a city is about people, and not defined by its buildings or skyline–those come later. Park's attempt to understand the root causes of the problems in Seoul and find creative solutions to them can be emulated in any metropolis.

Third, and the most basic conclusion: cities need someone to run them, whom citizens can hold accountable. The Seoul city administration claims, on its website, that it is currently pursuing 286 projects, straddling all the usual important issues such as transport, education, health and energy, among others. Park says he has asked all his staff to make data available to the public. 'Transparency increases credibility and accountability,' he insists. Just these tenets could be a good beginning in thinking about how we shape our cities.

27 October 2013

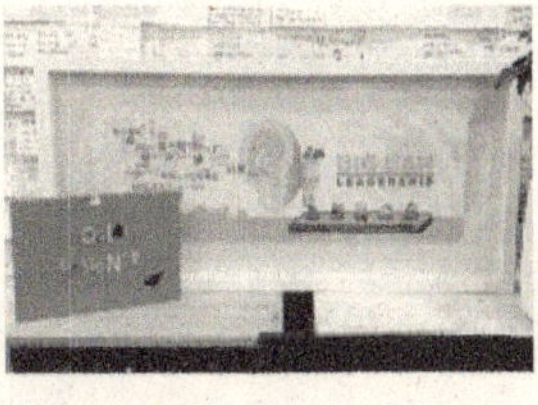

A cardboard placard saying 'Social Designer'

PERSONAL BRANDING

In a world dominated by fleeting digital media, the workplace provides an opportunity to express one's thoughts, beliefs and hopes with some degree of permanence.

This is especially significant in India. When entrepreneurs are the engines of the economy; workplaces of entrepreneurial businesses reflect the forces driving them. For example, stock market investor Rakesh Jhunjhunwala distills his views on investing and inscribes them across the office, from walls to coasters. Retail pioneer and Future Group chairman Kishore Biyani communicates his vision through a customized and crafted personal workspace.

Both offices serve as reminders that the physical environment can be an equally effective communication tool as a digital device, and much longer lasting.

The walls outside Kishore Biyani's cabin display his values

KISHORE BIYANI

THE ENTREPRENEURIAL STORYTELLER

A ten-floor office in a business park in Mumbai's Vikhroli suburb is quite intriguing. Its occupant is Kishore Biyani, chairman of the Future Group of companies, which has interests in retail, insurance and other consumer businesses, with Big Bazaar and Food Bazaar as flagship retail brands. At first glance, there seem to be two distinct, and somewhat contradictory, stories at Biyani's workplace.

With a fully fitted conference room instead of a large desk, this is one of the most progressive chief executive suites I've visited. Biyani sits at a square, eight-seater table, surrounded by a glass marker board, a white flipboard and a flat-screen TV. It is a work setting suited to collaborative discussion, technology-oriented debate and a non-hierarchical working style.

A gift from a friend signifying new ideas

Although there's a tiny desk in the corner of the room with a computer, Biyani prefers to work off the meeting table, surrounded by stationery and gadgets. 'You have a board here, and you have a board here, so you can work much better this way,' says Biyani, pointing. It is also the only workplace I've visited where the occupant's email

'Positivity, energy levels, simplicity–most of our values are reflected somewhere in this office.'

address is printed on the glass door; an interesting extension of the 'open-door policy'.

Yet it is more traditional than I expected. Although C-suites have generally been shrinking over time, Biyani's office is among the largest I've visited, 'almost as big as a two bedroom apartment', he jokes. Next to the table is a generous set of sofas and armchairs, with enough room left to wander comfortably around the office.

'The building floor plate is large, and we decided to keep the rooms big,' he explains, adding that the tenth floor is reserved for 'decision-makers and thinkers', and was thus labelled 'Vichaar'. These 'decision-makers' include family members and senior executives.

'Whoever has come to the tenth floor has arrived,' he says, suggesting a level of exclusivity and privilege that is fast fading in many workplaces. The decor, however, is frugal. Biyani emphasizes, 'We kept the office very simple and cost-effective, and didn't use any expensive materials.'

Narrative workplaces

What really distinguishes Biyani's cabin is not the size or furniture layout but the fact that it is a great example of 'narrative' C-suites. A chief executive's workplace can be classified into several categories, and a 'narrative' workplace is one that serves as a communication tool, telling stories about people and organizations.

This office has been crafted to reflect the retailer's personal beliefs, values and priorities. 'Positivity, energy levels, simplicity–most of our values are reflected somewhere in this office,' he says. Some of this is literal–the wall outside the cabin has a collage of values.

A life-size product display

Inside, the message is more metaphorical. Instead of large paintings, there is a floor to ceiling display of his products. A facing wall has portraits and inspirational quotes from a curated selection of world leaders, including Steve Jobs, Mahatma Gandhi and Mother Teresa. The last panel in the collage is a mirror, where anyone can see themselves–a clever twist, suggesting that anyone can aspire to be a world leader, and subtly reinforcing Biyani's own self-made roots.

'I found the legacy of emperor Ashoka's "second innings" very interesting. I want to live the second innings legacy more than the first innings.'

Finally, a series of awards line the windows. Only one of them really matters to him–'the international retailer of the year' awarded to Pantaloon Retail India Ltd (his flagship retail chain at the time) in 2007 by the National Retail Federation, a US-based association. 'It was a really big gathering, it is an international award,' Biyani says.

Theatre of retail

The combination of the life-size product display, the portraits of world leaders, the line of awards and the unconventional furniture, makes this C-suite layout almost theatrical–it has a distinctive atmosphere that most retailers strive to create to make their stores unique.

For me, Biyani's particular brand of theatrical

'You can't be static in a retail business. In the retail business, you should keep paddling.'

storytelling has three elements to it. First, originality. Since he pioneered large-format retailing in the country, Biyani earned a reputation as an industry maverick. Now, as he continues to grapple with the troubling after-effects of an economic slowdown on his business, and has to compete with a new breed of e-retailers, he knows he has to stand apart to thrive.

'I found the legacy of emperor Ashoka's "second innings" very interesting. I want to live the second innings legacy more than the first innings. I've already written the book about the first innings,' he says, referring to his autobiography, *It Happened In India* (2007), which documents his journey as India's retail pioneer.

Biyani's maverick spirit extends to questions related to Future Group's sizeable debt, routinely raised by media and research analysts (as of 31 March 2014, Future Retail, the group's biggest company, had a debt of ₹ 6200 crores, which remains high despite a rights issue in January 2015).

He unequivocally dismisses this. 'You are growing either out of debt or out of equity. Equity is more expensive, everybody says so. So why are people so concerned about it? I never understand why people ask this question. You can't be static in a retail business. In the retail business, you should keep paddling. So I don't understand, was there any other way to grow?'

An award for retail excellence

Second, Biyani's narrative hinges on audacity, as highlighted by the product display in his cabin. 'I believe I have an opportunity and chance to be bigger than any other food company in the country. Nobody in India must have even imagined the dimension in which I am thinking. If somebody can imagine what I have thought, I can reward him. That is the scale (on which) I am thinking,' he says.

'I have treated my food business as a kitchen for my stores. And I want to make everything that my store sells. So I have created a 110-acre "kitchen" (or, in other words, a 110-acre food park to manufacture a wide range of products to be sold at his upcoming convenience stores). The stores will be 1000-2500 sq. ft each, and I want to open 5000 of them, and 80 per cent should be my own products,' he says, adding that he is motivated by the unusually large scale of operations and high levels of integration. 'What else can I do? You only do what you know.'

'I think I am relevant because I am interested in many, varied subjects and disciplines. You can become irrelevant in a year if you are not able to understand what's changing.'

Finally, Biyani's narrative is noteworthy for its variety, just like the diverse use of images, text, display and graphic media in his office. Drawing from spirituality, history, mythology and more, he has adopted a variety of storytelling techniques to talk about himself and the business, both within the company as well as with external stakeholders.

But he doesn't delve deep into any of these subjects. 'I never went deep into spirituality and mythology. It is not my place to go so deep into anything that I might drown in it. I think I am relevant because I am interested in many, varied subjects and disciplines. You can become irrelevant in a year if you are not able to understand what's changing.'

Like any piece of storytelling, there are audiences who might walk out unconvinced, and others who will keep coming back for more.

22 February 2015

Portraits of world leaders with inspirational quotes

RAKESH JHUNJHUNWALA

Jhunjhunwala monitors market movements and investments through several trading screens on his large, custom-made desk

THE DISTILLED CAPITALIST

Rakesh Jhunjhunwala's private office embodies the fabled stock market investor's dream. A corner room with an AstroTurf terrace garden, it overlooks a glimmering Arabian Sea. It is a peaceful sanctuary for quiet reflection, in contrast to any financial carnage that may be taking place on the five computer screens on his desk.

Jhunjhunwala, particularly over the last decade, has carved a reputation for himself as one of India's wealthiest and most astute stock market investors and traders.

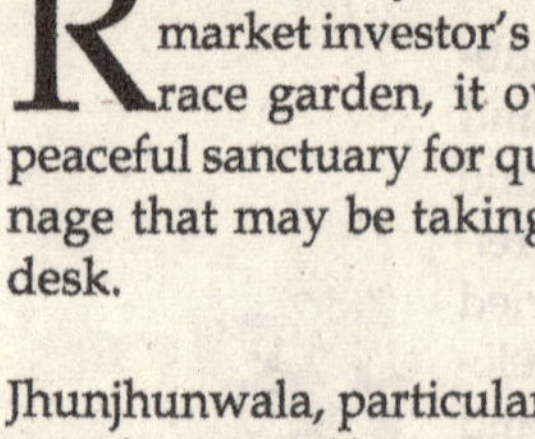

A glass bull, given by a friend, reflects the popular perception of his investing style

His investment firm Rare Enterprises has had a 5550 sq. ft workspace, located on the fifteenth floor of Nariman Bhavan in Mumbai's Nariman Point since 2004. He moved there from a compact space in Vithaldas Chambers, also in Nariman Point, when the firm needed to expand. The present location is, quite literally, vertically removed from his start 'on the pavement outside the stock exchange' in 1986, as he describes it.

'I need a sense of achievement; I want to earn the greatest wealth of the world with the greatest practical integrity and give as much as possible to charity.'

Jhunjhunwala's tastefully appointed rectangular room has lounge seating for visitors and an eight-seater meeting table. Colleagues are seated outside in adjoining cabins, in a trading room, and in open-plan workstations.

And that is where the resemblance between most corporate offices and Jhunjhunwala's workplace ends. Rare Enterprises' office design and layout speak volumes about its chief occupant. In fact, the office has been personalized to an extent not seen in most workspaces.

Personalized imprints

First, the desk. Like many senior managers, Jhunjhunwala sits at an imposing desk, which is nearly three metres long and over one metre wide. However, unlike most chief executives, the hefty desk serves a purpose beyond conveying authority. Five computer monitors placed on it enable Jhunjhunwala to simultaneously monitor his 'equity portfolio, smaller investments, trading positions, futures and Bloomberg'. It is his 'workplace', he says, laid out in a space-efficient way.

Most managers conduct meetings across a table, but Jhunjhunwala turns his back to his desk during our conversation; a gesture as informal as his descriptions of himself. 'I'm very forthcoming and open,' he states, admitting during the course of the conversation 'I have very bad habits, I smoke at least twenty to twenty-five cigarettes a day, drink four-five large pegs of whisky a day.' He is equally candid about his approach to wealth creation, stating that 'I need a sense of achievement; I want to earn the greatest wealth of the world with the greatest practical integrity and give as much as possible to charity.'

His personal workspace is divided into two work settings, with a conference table to meet visitors

Hand-drawn sketches and words of wisdom from stock market gurus such as Warren Buffett and George Soros are scattered through the office. Jhunjhunwala's opinions feature prominently on the walls of his cabin, in the form of 'ten commandments on investing and trading'. 'Take a loss. The first loss is the best loss,' I read, and 'It's important what you buy, it's more important at what price you buy.' Even the coasters are inscribed with advice; certainly the most idiosyncratic approach to office decor I've come across so far.

'Take a loss. The first loss is the best loss. It's important what you buy, it's more important at what price you buy.'

Jhunjhunwala's views are as distilled as his choice of evening beverage. More than any senior manager I've met, he has packaged his professional learning into pithy one-liners, on investing, and life in general. 'I think the most important thing I've learnt in life is that all adjectives are transient' or 'the hunt is more enjoyable than the kill', he tells me. I am even shown a handbook titled *My Investment Approach*, with a curated collection of quotes and anecdotes from varied sources.

The quotes reflect his curiosity, his desire to learn from reading and observing others, and his penchant for sharing his thoughts. 'I'm a thinking person,' he says. While he acknowledges the value of expert knowledge, he stresses the supremacy of independent decision-making. 'Everybody's chemistry of success and failure is different,' he professes. 'You cannot make money on borrowed mortgage.'

'I'm a thinking person. I think the most important thing I've learnt in life is that all adjectives are transient.'

His humour can be self-deprecating. 'Even twenty years ago,' he says, 'when no one was ready to listen to me, I used to give everyone my advice.' (The tongue-in-cheek humour extends to the rarely used office gym, outside which a sign reads, 'We pray that this room remains the best utilized part of this office for our true prosperity.')

Divinity and family gospel

Finally, there's the visible presence of close relationships. A row of Ganesha statues, all gifts from friends and business associates, are lined up against a wall. Apart from photographs of his wife and children, there is a prominent portrait of his late father, a man he continues to revere. A painting of the stock exchange depicts him chatting with old friend Radhakrishna Damani–'a person I consider my guru', he says.

He reads out a poem dedicated to his wife Rekha, cites his father's childhood gospel, and tells me he gets in to work at 1.30 p.m. on most days, after spending the morning at home with his family. Both his brother and brother-in-law have their own cabins in the office. Family clearly matters to Jhunjhunwala, yet he is categorical about remaining 'ruthless in business' and 'emotionless in leverage'.

A painting of the Mumbai Stock Exchange and Jhunjhunwala with his long-time friend, Radhakrishna Damani

Do close family bonds provide the foundation for his maverick spirit? I wonder. 'Being practical and grounded not only helps in investing, it helps very much in the outlook on life,' he agrees.

'Being practical and grounded not only helps in investing, it helps very much in the outlook on life.'

This approach extends to his cabin; he likes it for 'its peace and quiet', not for its spectacular view or the terrace garden.

Although Jhunjhunwala is often called 'India's Warren Buffett' by the media, Rare Enterprises is not an institution like Berkshire Hathaway. Its founder is also not bothered by the fact that so many try to emulate his actions. If anything, the office captures a slice of Indian entrepreneurial capitalism: self-made, individual-led, secured by strong family ties, paternalistic, peppered with folk wisdom.

By remaining the centre of operations, he has also freed himself from worrying about succession. 'I don't want my children to do what I choose for them. The modern world is all about human right and human choice. Maybe Rare will die with me, what's wrong?' Another ode to independence.

27 May 2012

STORYTELLING

The power of space, as a narrative medium, is beginning to manifest itself in corporate India, with digital companies leading the way.

At fashion Internet retailer Myntra.com, chief executive Mukesh Bansal is surrounded by images of fashion legends, and a life-size mannequin display at the reception. Dippak Khurana, the chief executive of mobile advertising exchange platform, Vserv.mobi, uses the digital metropolis as a branding device to communicate the company's service offerings. Tech entrepreneur Amar Goel's global start-up Komli Media has writable walls and more conference rooms than most, to facilitate non-stop collaboration and global connectivity, an essential element of its customer service offering.

Narrative workplaces are especially evident at the local offices of some iconic global brands. Rajiv Mehta, the former managing director of Puma's Indian operations, imbibed the brand's joyfulness and energy through a sporty and irreverent workspace.

Similarly, at the corporate office of the Indian operations of iconic American motorcycle brand Harley Davidson, managing director Anoop Prakash enables brand purpose to filter through all aspects of the space. At music channel MTV, Aditya Swamy makes sure that the work atmosphere is collegiate, collaborative, digital and dynamic.

Management experts endorse storytelling at work. Stephen Denning, author of *The Leader's Guide to Storytelling* (2005), writes on Forbes.com that 'storytelling is a key leadership technique because it's quick, powerful, free, natural, refreshing, energizing, collaborative, persuasive, holistic, entertaining, moving, memorable and authentic. Stories help us make sense of organizations.'

It is particularly appropriate as a tool of workplace design, 'because it helps us deal with organizations as living organisms that need to be tended, nurtured and encouraged to grow. It thrives on inspiration rather than administration, fostering change rather than stasis,' he remarks. And perhaps most relevant of all–it does not have to cost a lot.

ADITYA SWAMY

Aditya Swamy, channel head, MTV, likes to work in the 'Vault'--a common meeting room

THE SOCIAL NETWORKERS

AMAR GOEL

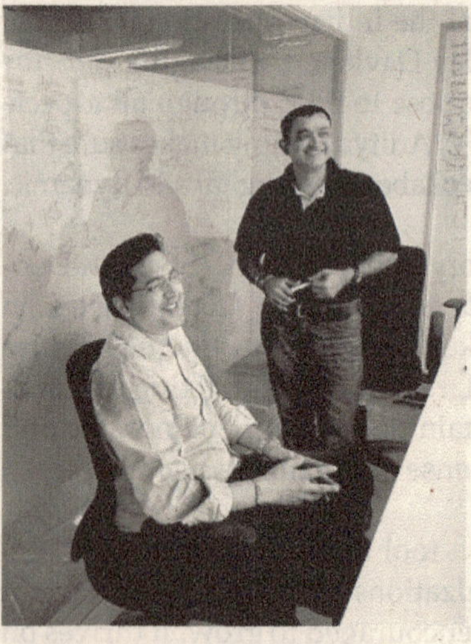

Amar Goel (seated) and Prashant Mehta of Komli Media work out of an open-plan office with writable walls in its meeting rooms

Sometimes, it really does make sense to pause and examine the writing on the wall. While visiting music television channel MTV's vibrant Parel office in Mumbai, I get some compelling insights into workplace design from an unexpected source: the walls.

This experience is echoed when I visit the Kalina, Mumbai, offices of Komli Media, an online advertising network founded in 2006 by Harvard computer science postgraduate Amar Goel.

Both companies are cut from the same cloth: they operate at the intersection of creativity, media, technology and youth. Komli

Walls are plastered with large vinyl stickers displaying MTV's current brand identity

Media serves as a digital media technology platform for Web publishers and advertisers. An iconic channel, MTV has morphed into a definitive youth brand, beaming across live events, mobile phones, the Internet and social media. The employee demographics of both companies are similar–an aspirational, energetic, tech-savvy and globally minded workforce, largely in its twenties.

'In tech, writing on the walls is kind of a cultural thing because engineers and product people want to write on whiteboards.'

Both are located in Mumbai's newer business districts–Komli Media occupies seven compact floors of a new high-rise commercial building in Kalina and MTV operates from a purpose-built, warehouse-like facility in Parel.

I am meeting their business heads, Aditya Swamy of MTV and Amar Goel of Komli Media, to get answers to something that has been intriguing me for some time: How does one successfully design a workplace for Generation Y? And how do the thirty-something CEOs of such companies operate in such environments? Are they cocooned from the rest of the office or fully integrated in the trenches?

The writing on the wall

Part of the answer, it seems, lies in the walls. At Komli, the walls are truly writable. Made of toughened glass and coated with a white film, all

'You've got to give team members logic and convince them, it's not just "hey, I'm telling you it won't work".'

the walls of the company's numerous meeting rooms are filled with scribbles. 'In tech, it's kind of a cultural thing because engineers and product people want to write on whiteboards,' explains Goel, chairman of Komli Media. Instead of conventional whiteboards, Goel and his colleagues preferred glass as a material, as it maximizes natural light penetration into other parts of the office.

At MTV, the walls (and cabinets) are dynamic, and branded. They are plastered with large vinyl stickers displaying MTV's latest brand identity: Stay Raw. Swamy, channel head, explains that since the brand adopts a new tag line every few years, vinyl stickers are the most effective way of updating the workplace without having to make major structural alterations. While the walls, and vertical surfaces, of any 'youthful' office are always quite lively, at both Komli and MTV they evidently play a visible role in reinforcing company culture.

Speaking to both business heads, one important similarity emerges. For these two CEOs, the notions of 'personal space' and 'public space' are almost interchangeable. Unlike most CEOs of an older generation, Goel and Swamy are comfortable working alongside other team members, in different parts of the office apart from their officially assigned spots. As a result, they relate strongly to the needs of their junior colleagues, and the design of the entire office is as relevant to their way of working as their private spaces.

Collaborative

The first point emphasized by both Swamy and Goel is the need to be collaborative in approach. Generation Y workers are more likely to question their bosses. Says Swamy, 'You've got to give team members logic and convince them, it's not just "hey, I'm telling you it won't work". As a result, offices must be physically open-plan, so as to maximize communication between colleagues. At MTV, only the heads of the three channels (MTV, VH1 and Nickelodeon), and the company head of Viacom 18 have cabins.

'It's all about taking action, fast, the whole style of long monthly review meetings is not my style.'

At Komli, no one has cabins, everyone has similar-sized workstations. Goel is seated adjacent to Komli's CEO, Prashant Mehta, separated by a low partition. Both Goel and Mehta eschewed private offices when designing Komli's office fit-out. Large, individual cabins were not 'justifiable' for a company of Komli's size, explains Goel. Natural light, better ventilation, adequate desk space and more meeting rooms were bigger priorities, he adds.

For discussions there are seventeen meeting rooms of various dimensions–a huge number, given that the entire office accommodates 180 people. Each floor has three meeting rooms, meant for internal team meetings. Apart from these, an entire floor is dedicated to meeting and conference rooms, some of which are larger and equipped for video, Web and phone conferencing.

As a 'global start-up' with offices in twelve locations across the world, virtual collaboration is a business necessity for Komli. 'Because we're spread across a lot of geographies, people are always on the phone with other people, and always trying to connect, there's a lot of team stuff,' says Goel, who himself shuttles between meeting rooms throughout the day.

Clean

The personal desks of both Swamy and Goel sport a similar, paperless, uncluttered look. This is as much the outcome of technology as a faster pace of work. 'It's all about taking action, fast, the

'Most of our people live and breathe with their computer. They take it to meetings, to presentations, they take it home, they take it on vacations. This is not their work computer, it's their life computer.'

whole style of long monthly review meetings is not my style,' says Swamy. Similarly, for Goel, writing notes on the walls comes more naturally than accumulating stacks of paper.

For both, their personal workspaces appear to have functional, rather than emotional, connotations. Swamy's office bares little traces of personalization, apart from a collection of 'access cards' to MTV events, which he saves as memorabilia, and a few MTV branded items. Goel's desk is similarly bare.

Collegiate

As expected, the spatial metaphor of the 'college canteen' travels seamlessly to both offices, in the form of beanbags, informal lounges and recreational amenities like a pool table or table tennis table. Both Goel and Swamy are comfortable in the casual environment–in fact, the beanbag in Swamy's cabin was one of the first additions when he moved into the space.

Equally, both are quick to highlight that while the offices might appear casual, it doesn't imply that people don't work hard. 'Nobody cribs about working twenty-four hours a day, four-five days in a row. They sleep here, we have showers and bunk beds,' testifies Swamy. Recreational amenities are thus seen as legitimate pay-offs for consistently long hours.

Contraptions

Gadgetry and technology, in the form of laptops, smartphones and the Internet, are vital in Generation Y offices. 'Most of our people live and breathe with their computer. They take it to meetings, to presentations, they take it home, they take it on vacations. This is not their work computer, it's their life computer,' Goel emphasizes. Both meeting rooms and workstations need to be wired for multiple technological gadgets. Swamy's need to stay current with media and music is evident in the three flat-screen televisions and impressive music system in his cabin.

Speed of decision-making, openness, informality and technology are important criteria when designing a 'youthful office'.

When designing workplaces for a younger workforce, clients and designers are usually fixated on bright colours and beanbags. Swamy and Goel's spaces and workstyles reveal that surface treatment is just part of the 'youthful office' story. Speed of decision-making, openness, informality and technology are equally, if not more, important criteria.

25 September 2011

UPDATE: *MTV has moved to the corporate office of its parent, Viacom 18 in northern Mumbai. Prashant Mehta left Komli in December 2013.*

A lectern allows Anoop Prakash of Harley Davidson to stand and work on his computer

ANOOP PRAKASH

THE EVANGELICAL EXPLORER

Every so often, I visit a corporate headquarters that wears its brand on its sleeve, where a closer look at the finer detail is almost unnecessary. This is one such example, a ground-floor office in Gurgaon, Haryana, occupied by Anoop Prakash, managing director of Harley Davidson's India operations, and his colleagues.

Harley branding, Harley motorcycle parts and Harley-inspired memorabilia dominate the walls, desks and partitions of this workplace. A collage of motorbike tanks frames the reception. There are bike handlebars on the washroom doors. Wooden jaali screens, with carvings of the Harley logo shields, separate the different areas of the office. And, of course, there are several actual bikes displayed in the training area. It is a fitting tribute to an over 100-year-old American brand that inspires a cult, and usually lifelong, passion among its customers.

Harley-inspired memorabilia on Anoop Prakash's desk

Flexible and personalized

Prakash moved to India from the US in 2009 to launch Harley. He and his colleagues moved into the current office space in May 2010, after several months of working out of a business suite in Gurgaon. 'Each Harley Davidson office around the world invokes our brand, values and heritage in its own unique way. So this is similar to others elsewhere, but unique,' says Prakash. He adds that they chose Delhi architects Morphogenesis, because 'it was going to be our home for a long time, and we liked their thoughtful approach'.

'Each Harley Davidson office around the world invokes our brand, values and heritage in its own unique way.'

The company's mission statement, 'We fulfil dreams of personal freedom', is displayed prominently in Prakash's office. For him, 'motorcycles are a form of self-expression'.

This is reflected in his unusually configured workspace, which embodies a distinct sense of personalization. His cabin-sized desk is located in an open office, with what looks like a height-adjustable lectern placed against it.

'Being located here in the open office gives me a sense of what's going on in the office. I feel the pulse of what's happening, with the conference room behind me, and the open space in front of me. If I see a partner coming in to meet one of my team, I can pop in and greet them,' he says.

The feeling of open space and camaraderie is mirrored in the office design through a series of high-backed sofas lined against some of the workstations. These semi-enclosed settings encourage structured or spontaneous group conversations, says Prakash–for example, when customer issues need to be tackled by pulling in different members of cross-functional teams from sales, operations and customer care. 'These are

The workshop and training room at the back of the office

full throughout the day; they have worked out really well,' he says.

'I enjoy standing and working, it keeps me energized, keeps me active.'

The lectern enables him to stand and work on his computer. Prakash says he began doing so last year, after reading about 'how sitting is so bad for you. I enjoy standing and working, it keeps me energized, keeps me active. If someone comes to meet me and they sit, then I'll sit down. What I like about the open office is that I can walk, see someone, I can ask questions,' he says. He also wears a fitness-tracking device from Jawbone on his wrist, to keep track of his daily footsteps.

Prakash's sense of discipline and commitment to fitness is unsurprising, given his background as a former US Marine Corps (he served as an intelligence officer in the helicopter squad for four years after graduating from college).

There are several pieces of Harley memorabilia on his desk–a box of Cuban cigars, the original sketches of a bike by a Harley designer, an old sake glass from the opening of the Harley office in Japan–as well as other personal items, including an amusing game to help one procrastinate at work. It was a gift from a friend, when he worked as a management consultant at consulting firm

McKinsey & Co. after completing his master's degree in business management from Harvard Business School in 2001.

'We fulfil dreams of personal freedom. Motorcycles are a form of self-expression.'

Riding new avenues

Exploration–both literal and metaphorical–is a key element of the Harley Davidson brand, and it is clear that building the brand in India entailed a big journey for Prakash.

'What attracted me to this opportunity was how challenging it appeared. India was the last frontier and was one of the largest two-wheeler markets in the world, yet it was defined by commuting and transportation, rather than leisure and recreation, when you think about the motorcycling market,' he says. 'A lot of change was happening. Harley executives were coming to India since the mid-1990s just to see what was happening in the market. And I think they saw some tremendous changes and we all felt that if we could time it right, we could be one of the first movers in the market and make an impact,' he adds.

Sales have kept pace with expectations, with 'high double-digit growth rate', says Prakash. 'As of now, we have crossed almost 8000 motorcycles on the road. And that's since we opened our first dealership in 2010,' he says. Prakash adds that some competitors have publicly acknowledged the growth of the premium motorbike segment due to Harley Davidson's Indian presence.

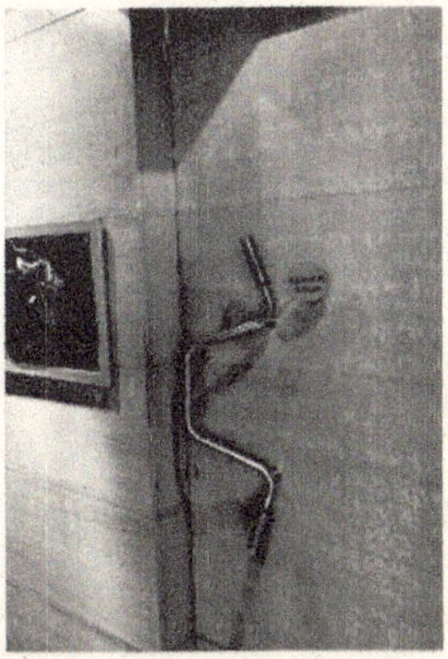

Motorcycle handlebars are used on doors in the office

The brand continues to engage with its customers and dealers in its hallmark 'rides'–group, multi-day cruises along highways and coastlines, whether in India or the US. Customers are invited to join the relevant

'We get a lot of feedback and understanding of how our products are performing, how our customers experience different road conditions.'

Harley Owners Group chapter that facilitates groups riding to destinations across the country. 'The most memorable ride I would say was our "western weekend" ride with both the Pune dealership and our Goa dealership on the same weekend, where we rode from Pune to Goa in a day. It was about a ten-hour ride. We went through the Western Ghats and down to Goa, cruising around. There was a lovely ride and we got nice sunset views. There were 5060 customers and about half a dozen other guys from the company in that particular two-day event. We get a lot of feedback and understanding of how our products are performing, how our customers experience different road conditions,' says Prakash.

His workplace may appear compact, premium and niche, but it offers a valuable lesson on how organizational mission, brand values and the work environment can be aligned with each other.

18 January 2015

Vibrant graphic design defines the offices of both Mukesh Bansal, co-founder and CEO of Myntra.com and Dippak Khurana, co-founder and CEO of Vserv.mobi

MUKESH BANSAL & DIPPAK KHURANA

THE DIGITAL MARKETERS

Two digital workspaces reinforce a long-standing design principle: Offices can be extremely effective platforms for brands to express themselves. And when a company's primary assets are virtual, its brick-and-mortar spaces must work even harder to communicate its brand values.

Usually, these values reflect the founder's beliefs. This is my conclusion after meeting the heads of two digital companies, Mukesh Bansal of Myntra.com and Dippak Khurana of Vserv.mobi.

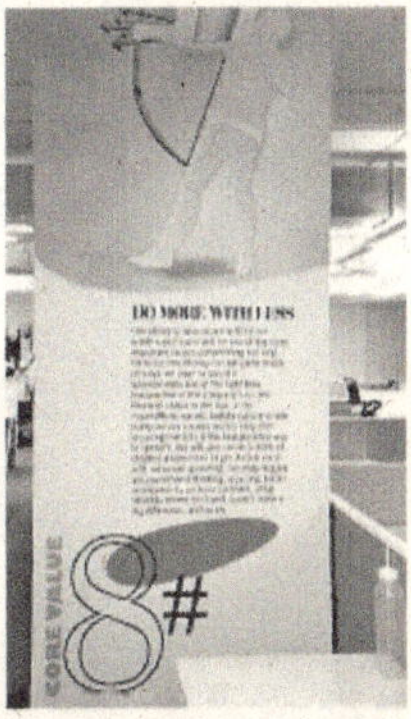

Myntra's core values are painted and illustrated on columns across the workplace

Office as a brand platform

Bansal is co-founder and CEO of Myntra.com, one of India's largest e-commerce companies, headquartered in an industrial estate off a busy highway on the outskirts of Bangalore. The gritty neighbourhood is an incongruous location for one of India's largest fashion e-tailers.

But perceptions begin to change at the reception.

Myntra's Bangalore office reception has a department-store-window-type display

Visitors are greeted with vibrant, department-store-window-type mannequin displays, showing off the latest in-house collections. The fashion theme continues inside the 30,000 sq. ft workplace–each of the company's fourteen meeting rooms is named, and designed, after a leading international fashion designer, such as Coco Chanel or Gianni Versace.

'We are very passionate about the business of fashion. The entire office reflects that.'

The 4000 sq. ft Mumbai head office of Vserv.mobi, a leading mobile advertising exchange, is more compact, but similarly crafted. The office address, on the ground floor of a bland corporate building close to the highway in Goregaon, is not particularly noteworthy. As one approaches the building, however, one can see a band of quirky characters wrapping the outsides of the ground floor in large vinyl stickers.

This set of mobile-themed characters is the company's signature branding element. It is present on office walls, on the company website, on Khurana's T-shirt and in his small, white-walled cabin, which lacks any other art or personal accessories, apart from a small shrine and some family photos. A tongue-in-cheek sign outside Khurana's room says 'Mayor', highlighting his role as the co-founder and CEO.

The fashion theme is carried through on all vertical surfaces

The characters depict a 'mobile city' and represent the 'the mobile ecosystem, which we love. This office has been conceived as a mobile city. My cabin is the Mayor's office, there is a hang-out area called the Mobizen Lounge and the boardroom is the House of Lords,' explains Khurana.

It is a memorable branding device that differentiates the company from its peers. The concept for the company's office space was first developed in partnership with Goa-based Beard Design, a visual communications firm. 'We realized that it was really helping build our brand, so we adapted it for employee T-shirts, the website and visiting cards,' says Khurana.

'We thought a lot about what kind of a culture we want in Myntra and what values we want, because an office space is an embodiment of an organization's beliefs.'

Bansal endorses this three-dimensional approach to branding. 'We are very passionate about the business of fashion. The entire office reflects that,' he says, adding that while thinking about how to design the office, 'we thought a lot about what kind of a culture we want in Myntra and what values we want, because an office space is an embodiment of an organization's beliefs'.

The company's core values, and business tenets, are painted and illustrated on columns across the workspace, urging employees to 'do more with

'All of us work from the same workstation, which was very important to us to symbolically communicate equality. We really, really believe in equality. No special things for senior management.'

less', 'work hard, play harder' or 'wow the customers'. The values are also expressed in the office layout, through the one-size-fits-all philosophy. 'All of us work from the same workstation, which was very important to us to symbolically communicate equality. We really, really believe in equality. No special things for senior management,' says Bansal.

He sits at an open-plan desk, just like everyone else, alongside a team of business analysts that works with him. When he needs to make private calls or have meetings, he just pops into the closest available meeting room. 'Hierarchies are not very conducive to productivity, as people don't speak up,' Bansal points out, highlighting that even lateral-entry senior hires from outside the company have adjusted easily to the more democratic work environment.

Multiplier benefits

Both entrepreneurs emphasize that creative workplaces meet strategic business objectives by serving as platforms for recruitment and business development as well as a motivational tool for employees.

Bansal is seeking to establish Myntra.com as one of the largest national fashion retailers–offline or online–in the industry. 'Last year, for the first time, we held a brand meet where we called the heads of national (fashion) brands. They were floored when they saw our office; their perception of the company and our relationship with the brand went to a different level,' Bansal says.

Mobizen Lounge, a break-out area at Vserv.mobi

Khurana aspires to be the leading emerging markets mobile exchange, connecting advertisers, app developers, publishers and telecom providers. Vserv.mobi is already a global start-up, with offices in six cities around the world,

Vserv.mobi's office in Mumbai has mobile-themed characters, the company's signature branding element, on its walls

apart from India, and it is important for it to be perceived as a transnational enterprise, independent of geography.

The contemporary, human 'mobile city' characters have a significant positive impact on potential new hires and customers, says Khurana. 'Today, when someone comes to our website, they see it matches any global standard,' he says.

Vserv.mobi's 'mobile city' characters make a significant positive impact on potential new hires and customers.

A creative concept originally intended for office design has now become a branding tool across various touch points. 'On any given day, up to a third of the office will be wearing the company-branded T-shirts,' says Khurana. The shared, casual look helps in getting people to open up, he says. It also impresses new recruits and potential hires, especially those from new geographies, who are encouraged to visit the office.

Consistent communication

What struck me was how strongly the office design correlates with Khurana's and Bansal's energy, passion and focus towards their businesses. Brands are often included in office interiors, but usually limited to just graphic images and surface-level treatments.

Each meeting room is named after a famous fashion designer

At Myntra.com, the founder's values and beliefs are expressed in a three-dimensional way, through space allocation and visual communication.

At Vserv.mobi, the founder's commitment to the mobile domain is constantly reinforced through online and offline touch points. Some lessons for all marketers, regardless of domain.

24 November 2013

UPDATE: *Vserv.mobi shortened its name to Vserv in September 2014 and evolved into a smart data platform. Myntra was acquired by Flipkart in May 2014, and has expanded to two new buildings, next to the original corporate office.*

Rajiv Mehta slides down from his rooftop cabin to meet his colleagues

RAJIV MEHTA

THE ECLECTIC ATHLETE

When some chief executives want to interact with their colleagues, they casually saunter around the office. Others prefer a more purposeful stride. Rajiv Mehta takes an entirely different route. The managing director of the Indian subsidiary of sports apparel brand Puma slides–literally. The fastest route between Mehta's rooftop cabin and that of his colleagues' is a red, fibre-reinforced plastic, Puma-branded slide.

The slide was an afterthought, explains Mehta. The office occupies several floors in a compact commercial building in Bangalore's Indiranagar. During the office interior fit-out, Mehta was allocated the topmost cabin, situated on the building's terrace roof, alongside the company's cafeteria.

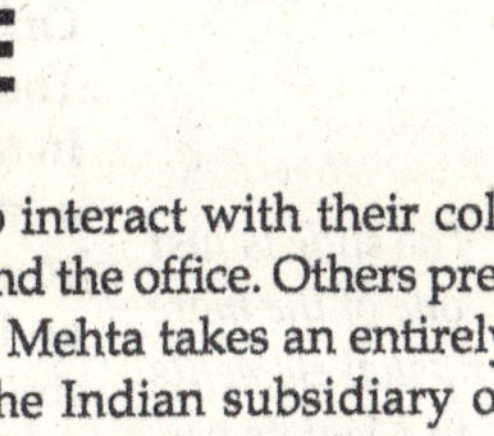

Graphics liven up the walls at work

Colleagues predicted that he would squander time and energy running up and down the stairs, as most of his day is spent in meeting colleagues, so he asked if the space could accommodate a slide. An existing ar-

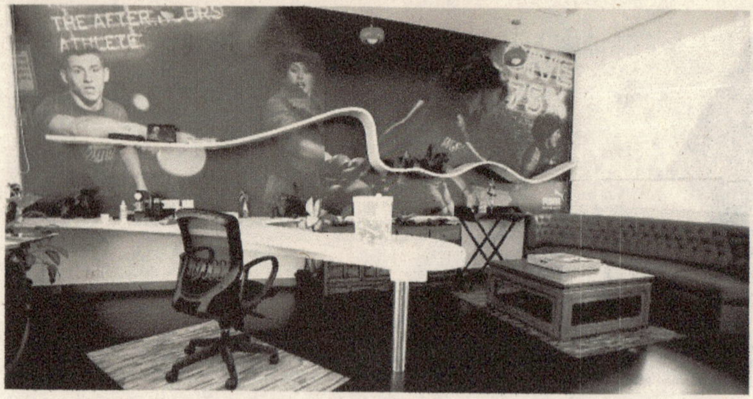

Rajiv Mehta's cabin has fluid lines and informal furniture

chitectural void in the space allowed a slide to be constructed without any structural change to the building interior. Mehta and his team use it regularly.

Office as living room

The slide is just one of the more unusual elements in Mehta's personal workspace. Mehta's cabin is a large space with two flowing desks and an equally fluid bookshelf. The desks are for him and 'his boss from Germany, who visits a few times a year and likes to sit in my cabin', he clarifies, adding that the amorphous lines were conceived by him and Puma's in-house architect, Payal Phadnis, to contrast with the rectangular geometry of the room.

The slide is just one of the more unusual elements in Mehta's personal workspace. The workspace resembles a living room or study–informal and personalized.

A curated assortment of furniture and furnishings decorate the room, built around the theme of 'a little bit of modern and a little bit of retro', says Mehta. There are leather rugs, a vintage-looking chest of drawers for papers, a hand-drawn cart serving as a magazine stand and a custom-made sofa, all sporting the brand's red and white colours. Slogans and visuals endorse sport; Mehta himself runs a few kilometres every morning. A particularly witty artwork by American artist Joey Roth captures typical office personality types in the form of shapes.

'We call ourselves the DJ who fuses sports and lifestyle very well. Joy and energy are very important elements of our work culture.'

Mehta says he likes assembling pieces from different sources, including relatively unknown designers and artists. As a result, the workspace almost resembles a living room or study–informal and personalized. The offices of those running small creative businesses often adopt this design approach; it is far less visible in the larger cabins of more corporate marketers, such as Puma.

Office as brand ambassador

Thc rest of the office is equally distinctive, reflecting Puma's athletic youth culture. Next to the slide is a rock-climbing wall and a punching bag. Conference room tables are derived from sports tables such as those for billiards and foosball. Hand-painted graffiti and cartoon art liven up the walls, with witty references to pop culture, such as 'Mere pass PuMa hai'. Workstations are open and stylized, with custom-designed task lighting.

The goal was to bring the brand philosophy into the workspace, says Mehta. 'We call ourselves the DJ who fuses sports and lifestyle very well. Joy and energy are very important elements of our work culture.' With a limited budget, the team relied on in-house expertise for the decor.

Office as hang-out zone

This philosophy extends to after-hours benefits too–employees can relax after work over a foosball table, in the cafeteria or in front of the gaming station. The company orders snacks for those working late. For Mehta, providing an energizing work environment is part of a broader talent attraction and retention strategy. Since most employees are single and less than thirty years old, he says they appreciate being able to hang out at

Leisure options include several games and sporting activities

The design of the office underlines other aspects of managing a younger workforce, which is prepared to work hard, and in return, expects 'fairness and respect for one's individuality'.

the office with their colleagues after work.

The workplace's pronounced emphasis on leisure and recreation prompts an obvious question–does anyone actually get any work done? Mehta acknowledges that there are inefficiencies, such as elongated lunch or coffee breaks, unlike in the Western world, where 'one hour means one hour, you'll get back to work; coffee break means five minutes, and you'll get back to work'. He strives to ensure that Puma's informal work culture is balanced with a regular schedule of meetings where deliverables and timelines are monitored.

The design of the office underlines other aspects of managing a younger workforce, which is prepared to work hard, and in return, expects 'fairness and respect for one's individuality. I cannot demean them, they need affirmation,' says Mehta. It is a give-and-take approach, and entails balancing power with persuasion.

There are other challenges of working with a more wired generation–attention spans are often shorter, especially in meetings. But equally, young people can be quicker at processing information and making decisions, notices Mehta.

Office of the future?

Vibrant, lively, casual and recreational–is Puma's workspace an indication of a future direction for Indian workspaces?

Its approach is more likely to be echoed in creative organizations such as advertising agencies, rather than mainstream marketers.

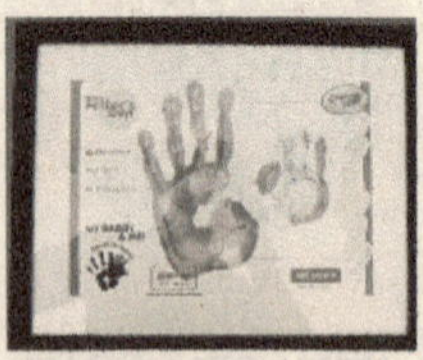

Children's artwork in Mehta's cabin

Mehta is clearly younger and has also been in the job for longer than most chief executives–for seven years, starting 2005, when Puma sales in India were negligible. Youth and job longevity is

Sports tables have been converted into conference tables, like this pool table

an unusual combination, and helps to explain how his team and he have translated the Puma sporting spirit into spatial design.

Now, Puma is no longer the start-up it was when Mehta joined them. Although Mehta says he cannot share sales figures, he says the brand has a 25 per cent share of the ₹ 2000 crore sports footwear, apparel and accessories market.

As the company expands its business and its headcount, it will be interesting to see whether its workspace retains its physical elements, and its quirky sense of humour.

His aim is to establish Puma as a leading apparel brand, especially given that competitors Reebok and Adidas are embroiled in an ongoing controversy relating to accounting fraud at Reebok's Indian subsidiary.

As the company expands its business and its headcount, it will be interesting to see whether its workspace retains its physical elements, and its quirky sense of humour.

7 October 2012

UPDATE: *Rajiv Mehta left Puma in September 2014; the slide remains.*

SECTION IV: ENVIRONMENT & SUSTAINABILITY

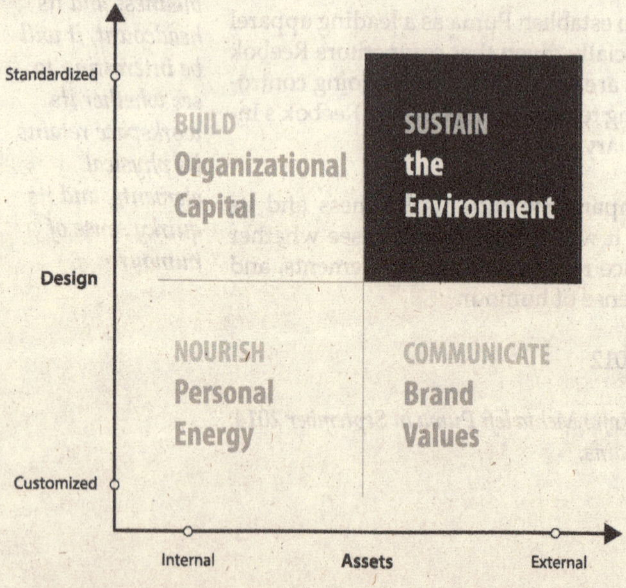

SUSTAINABILITY

Buildings are silent but deadly assassins when it comes to environmental degradation, due to the magnitude of resources needed to construct, operate and maintain them.

Although the green building movement has attracted many followers in India, and rating systems such as LEED (Leadership in Energy and Environmental Design) have become more popular, only a few chief executives brought up the environment as a specific aspect of their business, their way of working or leadership approach.

Meher Pudumjee, chairperson of engineering company Thermax, stands out for her personal embodiment of 'green' values. For her, frugality is a mindset, a way of working and a physical state; the essence of sustainability.

Douglas Baillie, chief human resources officer for consumer products multinational Unilever, adopts 'agile working' to reduce carbon footprint, as part of Unilever's global mission statement for 'sustainable living'.

Hopefully, they will be less of a minority in the future.

DESIGN TRIGGERS FOR A 'SUSTAINABLE' WORKPLACE:

1. *Would you like to make provisions to:*
   a. *use less water in your facility?*
   b. *optimize use of energy?*
   c. *conserve natural resources?*
   d. *generate less waste?*
2. *Would you be willing to invest in new technologies and ways of working to reduce travel, communication and real estate costs?*
3. *Would you like to leverage workplace design to encourage employees to work in a more sustainable way?*
4. *Would you like to know more about how an existing facility can be redesigned to make it more sustainable?*
5. *Do you believe 'sustainability' goals can be aligned with business goals?*

Baillie divides his time between Unilever offices in London, Kingston upon Thames and Rotterdam

DOUGLAS BAILLIE

THE AGILE ATHLETE

Once again, the *Head Office* interview is not taking place in a 'corner office'. Instead, I am being taken to a lounge-style meeting room at Unilever House, a landmark, 1930s stone-clad building in central London, occupied by the eponymous Anglo-Dutch consumer products company. My subject is the company's chief human resources (HR) officer, Douglas Baillie, who also served as chief executive officer of Hindustan Unilever Ltd from 2006-08–and was responsible for conceiving the company's innovative corporate headquarters facility in Mumbai.

On the run

After a few minutes of discussion with Baillie, it becomes apparent that unlike previous occasions, it was not concerns about privacy that prevented me from being invited to his cabin for our conversation. The reason was slightly harder to comprehend. 'I work in a very agile way, so I don't have an office. I just find a desk... an office might be free like this at the moment, I plonk

A green bowler hat and family photos are among the few personal items in the office

'I work in a very agile way, so I don't have an office. I just find a desk... an office might be free like this at the moment, I plonk down.'

down. I'm just using this at the moment because it happens to suit,' Baillie says, taking me to his 'temporary office'.

It is a nicely appointed, glass-walled executive cabin that he uses whenever he is there; it has a large desk, a six-seater meeting table, bookshelves, cabinets and a great city view. Baillie adds that he usually divides his time between Rotterdam in the Netherlands, where he currently lives, and another large Unilever office in Kingston upon Thames in England, and uses any available space wherever he is.

Apart from electronic equipment and documents, there are not many personal possessions in this central London office–just a family photograph, a green bowler hat to celebrate St Patrick's Day, some books and a pair of running shoes. 'I'm in the process of moving out of a flat and moving from Holland to London, so I brought a few things with me to work as a place to store them temporarily,' Baillie says, pointing to the family picture. The office is used by other people when Baillie is not around.

The running shoes are a constant companion; Baillie is a veteran long-distance runner. 'The big one is next year–my tenth London marathon; I will be sixty years old and my three sons will run with me,' he says. And adds: 'Running for me is a stress-relief outlet. When there are lots of challenging issues to think about, I just go for a run. Then I get into a zone where I can really start thinking. It's a calming period, I usually come back very relaxed, I'm physically tired from the run and mentally tired from the strenuous day, and there's a balance,' he adds.

A new way of working

As a sponsor of the 'Agile Working' programme

Baillie's office is available for others to use while he's away

within Unilever, Baillie is leading a company-wide initiative towards a more flexible, technology-driven way of working. Unilever employees now have greater freedom to work from the location of their choice, are encouraged to collaborate with employees using videoconferencing, and are discouraged from travelling whenever possible to snip expenses as well as their carbon footprint. All the new or renovated facilities are designed to meet 'agile' standards, I am told, with greater spending on shared infrastructure rather than individual workstations and cabins.

All the new or renovated facilities are designed to meet 'agile' standards, with greater spending on shared infrastructure rather than individual workstations and cabins.

The aim is to make changes to three major enablers of work–facilities, technology and working practice–so that agile working can be an integral part of the environment, not equated with 'flexitime' or 'work-from-home' policies.

Greater spending on technologies to facilitate this way of working is compensated by lower spending on real estate, for agile offices typically have a smaller footprint than traditional offices. For example, they may have only seven workstations for every ten employees.

This sounds far removed from the Unilever I had experienced. Nearly ten years ago, I worked as

The view from Unilever House in London's Blackfriars neighbourhood

the strategic planner for an advertising agency in London, with Unilever Europe as a big client. My colleagues and I regularly flew business class to their Milan, Italy, office for two-hour meetings. Videoconferencing didn't seem to exist. It was old-fashioned and expensive even for its time.

The aim is to make changes to three major enablers of work–facilities, technology and working practice–so that agile working can be an integral part of the environment.

In her book *The Key: How Corporations Succeed By Solving The World's Toughest Problems* (2014), Lynda Gratton, a professor at the London Business School and a global human resources expert, highlights the importance of agility: 'Reducing (air travel and long commutes) required a complete redesign of the way that people work. This also brought home the realization that sustainability is not simply about natural resources, it's also about creating working practices that are energizing for people.'

Career moves

There are signs of agility in Baillie's personal career path too. A Unilever lifer, he worked in sales and marketing for most of his career, with several leadership positions in Africa, Asia and, most recently, in Europe. In February 2011, he was appointed the company's chief HR officer.

'I think I've always, in my career, been quite successful in developing great people and understanding leadership, so I was ready to have a go at it. My strength is that I can bring the business agenda to HR, rather than learning twenty-five years of HR,' he says, explaining his approach to the position.

Unilever's 'Sustainable Living Plan', a mission statement publicly shared by chief executive officer Paul Polman a few years ago, was an important driver for Baillie in taking on the new function. 'We work for a business that has a massive ambition. We want to double the size of our business, reduce our environmental footprint and make a positive social impact. The challenge for HR is, do we want to run behind the organization, filling in the cracks in the road as we go, or do we want to be a function that gets in front of the organization, and knows the road?' he asks.

'We work for a business that has a massive ambition. We want to double the size of our business, reduce our environmental footprint and make a positive social impact.'

This is an entirely new Unilever from the slow-moving giant I once knew, with its established processes, humdrum products and predictable advertising. Gratton endorses the company's new mission in her book. 'What Polman is attempting at Unilever is to lead the corporation down a path that is not a scramble but rather a more purposeful path . . . and a ten-year programme,' she writes.

As Baillie knows only too well, any long-distance runner needs discipline, determination and a sense of direction to achieve success.

14 September 2014

Unilever House is a landmark 1930s building

MEHER PUDUMJEE

Visitors to Pudumjee's office are welcomed with a print of folded hands, placed behind her desk. The desk belonged to her late father, Rohinton Aga, former Thermax chairman

THE FRUGAL EVANGELIST

This column begins with a query: What does the office of someone whose company advocates sustainability as a corporate mission look like? I've been speculating about this, as I've been keen to understand how environmental concerns reflect in work styles and workspaces.

A painting of horses which belonged to her late father Rohinton Aga

Meher Pudumjee, chairperson of Thermax Ltd, seems the ideal candidate. Her Pune-based engineering company professes to offer 'sustainable solutions for the energy and environment sectors'. The lesser-known fact, that this strategy seems to have worked–business revenues have tripled and profits nearly quintupled during her six-year tenure as chairperson–is an equally compelling reason.

'Clean and green'

As Pudumjee and I dissect her workspace, and discuss Thermax's 'clean and green' initiatives, a common vocabulary emerges, in her approach to the work environment and to saving the planet–frugality. The word summarizes three aspects: a physical state, a mindset and a way of working.

The Pune-based engineering company professes to offer 'sustainable solutions for the energy and environment sectors'.

Frugality and company chairmanship are unlikely companions, particularly in a family-driven business. Pudumjee's office certainly appears generous in scale, if not form. It is located on the fifth floor of the corporate office, adjoining the offices of the two other family members involved in Thermax–husband and director Pheroze, and mother and former chairperson Anu Aga. Pudumjee concedes that 'the openness sometimes feels over the top', explaining that the corporate office, completed in July 2008, was a long-awaited departure from the past–Thermax had previously always rented its facilities.

Although the office offers substantially more breathing room than many C-suites, it is a forgivable offence, given Pune's relatively lower real estate costs. The square foot to headcount ratio for employees is also higher than most office buildings. The educational NGO Akanksha, which is supported by Thermax in a number of ways, occupies 1771 sq. ft for its office, situated on the ground floor of the same facility.

If anything, the office's abundant square footage serves to highlight the rather unassuming collection of furniture and objects within Pudumjee's workspace. Collated for their personal appeal, rather than monetary worth, the possessions reflect their occupant's thrift. Pudumjee's desk belonged to her late father, Thermax chairman and company icon Rohinton Aga ('it has great sentimental value for me').

A Florentine mask

The walls are either bare ('I'm still looking for a painting to put up') or decorated with paintings by amateur artists, including early works by her

The spacious office is notable for its simplicity in layout, furniture and decor

two adolescent children, Zahaan and Lea. A print of two folded hands, sent by a family friend, sits behind her desk, a symbol 'welcoming visitors to my office' and 'almost a thing of gratitude'. The only flourish appears to be a 'beautiful' Florentine mask, acquired during a recent trip to Italy.

Frugality represents a physical state, a mindset and a way of working.

The understated decor echoes Pudumjee's approach to instilling a green consciousness in her company, which she says requires 'a mindset of frugality, not wanting to waste and also looking at it as an opportunity–any form of waste, how we can make something out of it'.

Converting waste to energy is a thrust area for Thermax, alongside its established line of boilers and chillers, and a cause championed personally by Pudumjee. As an example, she describes the detailed process by which Thermax converts putrid municipal sludge to energy, having devised a 'spent-wash boiler, which not only destroys the odour and the waste, but makes something useful'.

Attention to detail appears to be a key element in Pudumjee's strategy to build a sustainable enterprise. For example, the Thermax corporate office is a silver LEED-rated (Leadership in Energy and

Terrace gardens enhance the corporate headquarters' green quotient

Environmental Design) building–an increasingly popular standard for new corporate buildings.

Unlike her peers, Pudumjee is unusually familiar with the rating's fine print. I am told that the building is constructed from fly-ash bricks, which are derived from 'waste from coal-fired power plants', and 8000 litres of water is recycled every day, of the 12,000 litres consumed in its washrooms and kitchens.

Being green implies 'a mindset of frugality, not wanting to waste and also looking at it as an opportunity–any form of waste, how we can make something out of it.'

Although there is an automated building management system to conserve power, she has noticed a flaw, complaining 'that the lifts have not been synchronized to save energy' and that when she presses the button for the lift, the one which is furthest away from her floor opens up before the lift which is closest.

Her observations remind me of a comment by legendary Indian architect B.V. Doshi, the founder-director of some of India's best known design schools at a lecture on design. Doshi emphasized that energy was historically considered sacred in India, and that architecture and planning were traditionally based on conserving energy of any kind–human, natural or artificial.

'Managing my time more effectively is something I've learnt hugely with the children being around.'

In a related sphere, maximizing existing resources is a theme that reappears in Pudumjee's day-to-day management style too, especially as a busy working mother. 'Managing my time more effectively is something I've learnt hugely with the children being around,' she affirms, recalling how she learnt to accomplish as much 'from 9.00 a.m. to 3.00 p.m.' (when she had to get out of the office and collect her first child from the babysitter) as she used to do 'from 9.00 a.m. to 9.00 p.m., before he was born'.

I wonder whether Pudumjee's almost strategic vision of frugality in corporate life can be acquired. The office's quiet confidence, her zest for spotting opportunities in waste products, and her precise time-management skills seem to be qualities inculcated over time.

Subscribers of the 'less is more' philosophy will certainly find it appealing.

16 January 2011

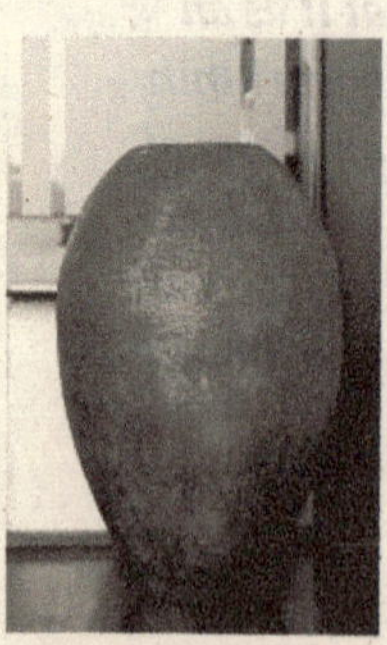

A locally acquired urn

ACKNOWLEDGEMENTS

When the origins of a book go back over a decade, there are many to thank, so I would like to express my gratitude in chronological order. This book explores the intersection between business and design, an interest that was first sparked when I was appointed chief executive of BP Ergo, my family's office furniture business, just a few months after graduating from business school in late 2002.

I realized quickly that my MBA curriculum omitted a necessary ingredient of my job: basic fluency in design management. Design informed every aspect of our business; from our ability to compete in the marketplace to the efficacy of our manufacturing and logistics operations, and I would first like to acknowledge the efforts of all my colleagues at 'Team Turbo Ergo' (as we called ourselves then), and particularly my senior leadership team, for educating me about design in a business context.

I also interacted with numerous design professionals during this time, including architects, interior designers, furniture designers, colour specialists, graphic designers and design engineers, and would particularly like to thank Christopher Sykes, Colette Austin, Kirti Trivedi, Latika Khosla, Neha Mital and Pradyumna Vyas for sharing their knowledge and expertise.

I am especially grateful to Radhika Desai, one of the finest interior architects I've met. Radhika and I first began writing about design more than ten years ago, every week, after work and on weekends; a partnership that endowed me with a design vocabulary and an enriched creative outlook. When we decided to publish our first case studies, it was a friend, Saumya Roy who introduced us to Elsa Eapen, my first editor at the *Mint*; to both of whom I owe an immense debt of gratitude.

The book is based on the monthly *Head Office* column published in the *Mint*, which was co-created with my formidable editor, Seema Chowdhry, whose rigour, clarity and discipline continue to be sources of inspiration, and who was also the first person to insist that I turn the column into a book.

Many colleagues at the *Mint* are responsible for crafting *Head Office* every month, including Manoj Madhavan, Preetha Kolore, Raajan Sharma, Sandipan Das and Saurabh Sharma from the photo team, and Chandrika Mago, Chanpreet Khurana, Nipa Chiragi, Pooja Singh and Tanushree Ghosh from the copy editing team.

I would also like to thank several *Mint* journalists and editors for sharing their perspectives whenever I have reached out to them, including Aniek Paul, Anil Padmanabhan, Gouri Shah, Niranjan Rajadhyaksha, P.R. Sanjai, Sapna Agarwal and Tamal Bandyopadhyay. A special thanks to *Mint* editor Sukumar Ranganathan for supporting both the column and the book, and to his executive assistant Bhavna Gupta for all her help over the last five years.

Fifty protagonists have been featured in *Head Office* so far, and many friends have generously shared their networks, their insight and their feedback to assist with interviews, including: Ajay Srinivasan, Ajit Ranade, Alok Kshirsagar, Apurv Bagri, Apurva Patel, Ashish Kumar Singh & Valsa Nair, Bharat & Vidya Doshi, Bhushan & Sheetal Gagrani, Chandra Iyengar, Fiona & Luis Miranda, Girish Kuber, Khozem Merchant, Leena Basrur, Leena Nair, Louise Pulford, Madhu

Kannan, Mala & Subramanian Ramadorai, Manjeet Kripalani, Namrata Kamdar, Niloufer Lam, Nitin Deshmukh, Pallavi & Pankaj Tibrewal, Pragnya Ram, Rajeev & Valencia Gupta, Raman & Geetanjali Deshpande, Ritesh Sharma, Sanjay, Shanu & Naman Pugalia, Sarita Hegde, Shilpa Rane, Shweta Khanna, So Jung Rim, Suvir Sujan, Tara Mahadevan and Tarun Chauhan.

At Penguin Random House, Milee Ashwarya and Caroline Newbury have championed the book from inception. Several friends also helped tremendously in turning the column into a book–Padmini Mirchandani who first urged me to do so, Anil Khandelwal, Lynda Gratton and Snehal Shah whose invaluable management insight and prompt feedback have made this a much better read, and book designers Shaifali Chikermane and Cathy Chen for whose patience, diligence and creativity I am extremely appreciative. I would also like to express a special thanks to Anand Mahindra for contributing a foreword to the book and to Prithviraj Chavan, whose interest in design is a source of inspiration.

Closer to home, I am deeply grateful to my domestic staff, including my children's nanny Champadevi Paswan and my housekeeper Ram Singh Saini, without whom I would not be in a position to write. I would also like to thank my research assistants and fellow work-from-home mothers: Roxanne Maben and Gayatri Kotikalapudi for their seamless and consistent support over the years; evidence that remote working works well.

I am blessed with a large, loving and supportive family; immediate as well as extended, for which I am deeply grateful, including Avinash & Asha Raje, Dilip & Shalini Piramal, Urvi Piramal, Ajay & Swati Piramal, Mukesh & Ruchi Kejriwal, Radhika Piramal & Amanda Meade, and Amartya & Agastya Raje.

Finally, there are two individuals without whom this book would not have been possible, and for whom any form of thanks cannot begin to capture the depth of my love, gratitude and affection: my mother Gita Piramal and my husband Amit Raje.

ANSWERS TO WORKPLACE QUIZ

1. Deepak Parekh
2. Rajiv Bajaj
3. Cyril & Vandana Shroff, Neera Nundy & Deval Sanghavi
4. Anoop Prakash, Rajan Anandan, Shantanu Khosla
5. Uday Kotak
6. Rajiv Mehta
7. Ajay Piramal, Meher Pudumjee, Natarajan Chandrasekaran
8. Ajay Piramal, Kumar Mangalam Birla, Vysyaprath Sunil & Mohit Dhar Jayal
9. Anoop Prakash, Rajan Anandan
10. Aruna Jayanthi, Natarajan Chandrasekaran

PHOTO CREDITS

Abhijit Bhatlekar
Aniruddha Chowdhury
Bhaskar Dasgupta
Devendra Parab
Indranil Bhoumik
Harald Haugan
Hemant Mishra
Jagadeesh N.V.
Kedar Bhat
Manoj Patil
Mithila Joshi
Nayan Shah
Pradeep Gaur
Priyanka Parashar
Seoul Metropolitan Govt
Susan Young
Vikas Munipalle

ABOUT THE AUTHOR

Aparna Piramal Raje writes regularly on business and design, workplaces, cities and urbanization for the *Mint*, India's second largest business daily, and the UK's Financial Times Weekend, a leading global publication. She has also co-authored a comprehensive report on the Indian design industry for the Confederation of Indian Industry (CII), and has worked as a television anchor for a leading business news channel.

Aparna was previously CEO of BP Ergo, one of India's largest office furniture companies, and has also worked with VIP luggage, one of India's best known consumer brands. She currently serves on the board of Kokuyo Camlin, one of India's largest stationery companies.

She completed an MBA from Harvard Business School and read Economics, Politics and Philosophy at Oxford University. She lives in Mumbai with her husband and their two sons.

She invites readers to email her at aparna@aparnapraje.com and to visit her website at www.aparnapiramalraje.com.